A SMALL TOWN AT WAR

1917 IN MID SUSSEX

Alan Miller

PUBLISHED BY
CUCKFIELD PARISH COUNCIL
QUEEN'S HALL
CUCKFIELD
WEST SUSSEX

COPYRIGHT 1999
ALAN MILLER

ISBN 0 9530348 1 X

Profits from this book will go to the
Queen's Hall Restoration Fund

Typeset by Dijiset Typesetting. Tel: 01444 870882.

CONTENTS

PREFACE — 5
ACKNOWLEDGEMENTS

1. **SETTING THE SCENE** — 9
   THE WAR SO FAR

2. **JANUARY-MARCH 1917** — 21
   THE SCENE CONTINUED – AT HOME
   THE WAR GOES ON

3. **APRIL-JUNE 1917** — 44
   MORE HOME EVENTS
   THE SPRING OFFENSIVE

4. **MEMORIES** — 60
   SCHOOLGIRLS REMINISCE
   FASHION

5. **JULY-SEPTEMBER 1917** — 65
   SUMMER AT HOME
   THE DITTY BOX
   THE MEMORIAL SERVICE
   THE SUMMER STORM

6. **OCTOBER-DECEMBER 1917** — 85
   AUTUMN, STILL AWAITING GOOD NEWS
   FATIGUE
   THE ROYAL SUSSEX REGIMENT

   EPILOGUE — 102

   INDEX — 106

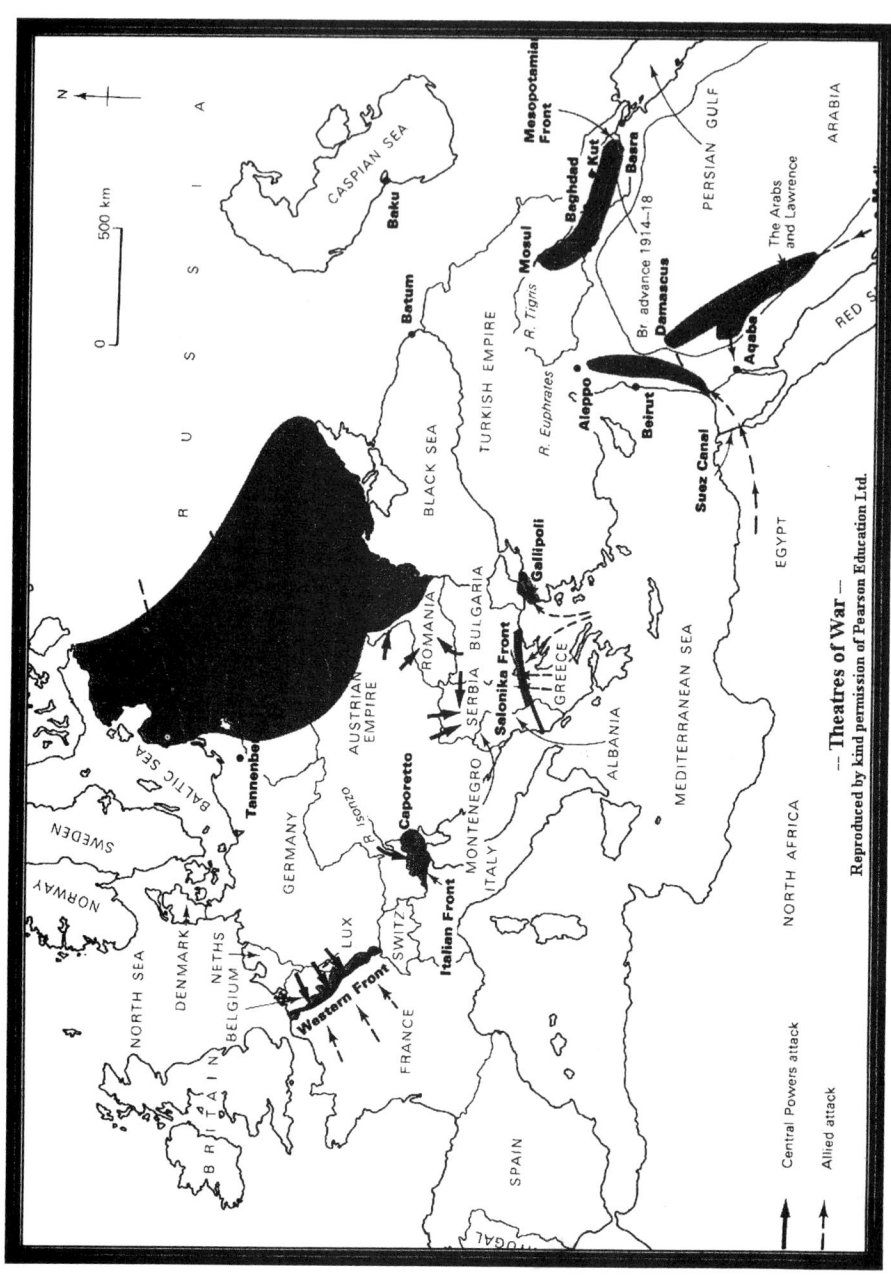

— Theatres of War —
Reproduced by kind permission of Pearson Education Ltd.

Preface

In this second book in the series one year in the life of, I have chosen to concentrate on 1917, twenty years on from "A Century Ago", which chronicled the life and times of the small town, Cuckfield, in late Victorian England. The Diamond Jubilee of Queen Victoria was the highlight of 1897. Once again, the small town of Cuckfield is the focal point of the story, which sees the year through the lives of its folk at home, with added stories from other towns and villages of Mid Sussex and their men and women.

In stark contrast to the generally happy picture of life revealed to the reader through the window into 1897, the year 1917 finds our forebears struggling with a more sombre set of circumstances.

I found the research absorbing and at times very sad. Certainly I became aware of peoples' perception of life. Expectations of the "classes" with their divergent regard for life are much different from today. So far have we travelled in the twentieth century, that the events of the second decade are next to impossible for us to comprehend, unless you have lived through it; some have.

City life during the war was fast. Men not in the Army or Navy and women gravitated towards the factories with the increased wages. Theatres were well patronised, there was an element of 'live for today'. 1917 was a sombre time; the war was in stalement. The toll on our fighting men was extreme. Hardships on the home front were hurting. Conscription was introduced in February 1916 with the Military Service Act, calling up men under forty-one, starting with those who had already voluntarily registered. Local tribunals were set up to decide a man's eligibility to apply for exemption. For many, their lives were severe.

As my research into the war grew I was drawn to the poetry of the time. Studying the work of several poets gave me a vital insight into the innermost feelings, thoughts and desires of the soldiers at war. As the war progressed so the poetry became more descriptive, more cynical perhaps, but certainly it has made a huge contribution to the history of the Great War. I have selected some pieces to add to the narrative where appropriate, hoping to give the reader a closer feeling for the mood of the men at the "Front", and perhaps for the people at home. I hope you enjoy my selection.

The constructive criticism of my reading team, Andy Revell, Derek Wood and especially Gabrielle Whyte for her knowledge of poetry, was much appreciated.

I am extremely grateful to Mr George Sassoon for allowing me to use Siegfried Sassoon's poetry. Also, thanks to the Estate of Edmund Blunden for "October 1914", reprinted by permission of the Peters Fraser & Dunlop

Group Ltd. Edmund Blunden was a pupil of Christ's Hospital School in Horsham. He was commissioned in the Royal Sussex Regiment and survived the war.

I am indebted to Lin Wood for allowing me to use some previously unpublished drawings and cartoons drawn by her father, Geoffrey Squire, and signed G.S., during the war. Falsifying his age, he was only seventeen, he served with the 290th London Brigade Royal Field Artillery. He was in France in 1916-1918. A pre-war student, he returned to college after the war and continued his studies, later becoming a successful freelance artist.

A special thank-you is due to the Editor of the *Mid Sussex Times*, Paul Watson. The extensive use of the Middy archives was invaluable. Also, of great help were the West Sussex Records Office, the Cuckfield Parish Church records and the Cuckfield Museum. The visit to the Royal Marines Museum was very stimulating, the curator Matthew Little's help in research into 1917, was much appreciated. Help with the history of the Royal Sussex Regiment was provided by Alan Redmond the archivist at County Records, Chichester, and Richard Callaghan the curator of the Regiment's Museum in Eastbourne. I value the permission given to use the Regiment's Badge and Colours. I should like to acknowledge the help given by the Author's Licensing & Collecting Society, the Design and Artist's Copyright Society and the Imperial War Museum for the photographs on pages 84, 95, 97 and 100. *Kelly's* Business Directory proved again to be most informative. Every effort was made in contacting the appropriate copyright owners.

Thanks to West Sussex County Council for support under their Parish Initiatives Fund; to the Mid Sussex District Council with their Information Partnership Grant Scheme; to the generosity of the Independent State of Cuckfield, the Cuckfield Society and the Cuckfield Parish Council, my publishers.

My reading to research the war led me to many books. Those that I found most helpful included the following:

The Macmillan Dictionary of the First World War. Stephen Pope & Elizabeth Wheal
The World Crisis 1911 - 1918. Winston S Churchill
Passchendaele, the Untold Story. Robin Prior & Trevor Wilson
The War the Infantry Knew. Captain J C Dunn DSO, MC and Bar, DCM
The Soldiers War. Peter H Liddle
Veterans - Last Survivors of the Great War. Richard Van Emden & Steve Humphries
The Experience of World War I. J M Winter
Twentieth Century History. Tony Howarth
The Great War - Documents from WSCC Records Office. Compiled by Kim Leslie
Mr Punch's History of the Great War.
Punch, or the London Charivari.

Poetry Books included:
The War Poems of Siegfried Sassoon. Rupert Hart-Davis
The Poems of Wilfred Owen. Edited by Jon Stallworthy
Some Corner of a Foreign field, Poetry of the Great War. Edited by James Bentley
Up the Line to Death, The War Poets of 1914-1918. Selected by Brian Gardner

    In acknowledging all the above, adequate words of praise and thanks are truly difficult to find.

    Finally, to Derek Wood, a friend and mentor for his encouragement and the loan of so many books for me to study, thank you. To Tom Wells, thanks for the Ditty Box. To Daisy Rhodes, Eva Malin, Winifred Woolven and Miss Dengate thank you for sharing your childhood memories. And, to my wife, Janet, I dedicate this book. She put up with my talking incessantly about it, and listened to my hopes and frustrations with wonderful patience.

Alan Miller - 1999

JOINING the COLOURS – Katharine Tynan

There they go marching all in step so gay!
  Smooth-cheeked and golden, food for shells and guns.
Blithely they go as to a wedding day,
                The mother's sons.

The drab street stares to see them row on row
  On the high tram-tops, singing like a lark.
Too careless-gay for courage, singing they go
                Into the dark.

With tin whistles, mouth-organs, any noise,
  They pipe the way to glory and the grave;
Foolish and young, the gay and golden boys
                Love cannot save.

High heart! High courage! The poor girls they kissed
  Run with them; they shall kiss no more, alas!
Out of the mist they stepped – into the mist
                Singing they pass.

OCTOBER 1914 – Edmund Blunden M.C.

From the white cottage on the glimmering wold
That sees the clustering village far away,
And hears no sound of life, the autumn day,
But tread of its own housewife hale and old;
And from the cottage in the fenland hold,
Where ancient gravel-pits are now the prey
Of slothful deeps and sedges withering gray;
And from the cottage in the orchard's gold –

From many-acred mansions they are gone,
And from the stithy, and the builder's shed;
By oast and rick and byre there linger on
Old men alone of bowed and hoary head.
While far away the lustful violence fails
Before the men from Britain's peaceful dales.

1

SETTING THE SCENE
THE WAR SO FAR

The Great War has been written about from every possible angle. Books proliferate chronicling all the major battles, regimental histories, personal recollections and so on. Without attempting to produce another such work, this book's purpose is to look at some effects of the war, on the lives of the people back home. It might, however, help to understand their feelings and what motivated them if we look at this chapter, as a layman's overview. Then, in subsequent chapters we review the war's actual progress.

In the decade before the outbreak of the war, Europe increasingly became a hotbed of expansionism. The empires of Germany, Austria-Hungary, Russia and Turkey (Ottoman), as well as such smaller countries as Serbia all had territorial ambitions. The Balkans were in turmoil and sides were drawn. France and Russia had sealed their allegiance in 1892. Germany confirmed its support of Austria-Hungary over the Serbian issue. Turkey joined their alliance. Britain initially remained outside the scramble for supremacy but its involvement became inevitable following guarantees to Belgium and France. Often considered as a significant factor to the cause of war was the Anglo-German race to build the best navy. However, its probable major effect was to help to achieve a worsening of diplomatic niceties. Britain was at that time the world's only true global power. It was very rich and had a huge navy, therefore, a much sought after ally. France was of course interested in recovering territory lost to Germany in 1871.

In the period leading up to the "war to end all wars", war was regarded as rather fashionable. Generals, Politicians and the Establishment were equally contributing factors in what had become inevitable. The coming war, was also considered and approved by the masses. There was an air of romanticism about war, tinged of course with patriotism. Anyway, most people thought it would be of very short duration. Patriotism was regarded as highly desirable, even character building.

Regardless of reason or high-minded ideals, the war began the scrabble for land, with a flurry of invasions. Germany invaded Belgium and France and France invaded Germany. Russia invaded East Prussia and Austria-Hungary invaded Serbia. In all the capital cities throughout Europe the outbreak of war was greeted with enthusiasm, patriotism and xenophobia. There was a belief by all that war would pave the way for a new order of things that would eventually benefit the world. Berlin failed to respond to a British ultimatum on August 4th concerning Belgium, thus war was declared on that day.

Britain had a large navy, the army was by comparison very small. There were about 250,000 regulars, of which about half were serving overseas; another half million were reservists and territorials. The British Expeditionary Force (BEF) was formed and within eight days the first units had landed in France. In Britain, volunteers came forward in droves, anxious to get out there before it ended without them. How little they knew! So, how did things go?

The strategy of land warfare was well established in 1914. It was based upon the precept that an army on the offensive would always overcome one preoccupied by defence. Germany had a large well-equipped army ready for an attacking role. Huge numbers of troops were transported to the front by train. They were then marched into battle with a vanguard of cavalry all highly trained and very mobile. Their early successes through Belgium and northern France fully justified this strategy. It was all rather similar to the Prussian offensive of 1870. The French in contrast, not so well prepared, failed with their invasion plans further south.

The BEF's first action was at Mons, the Battles of the Frontiers. They expected to meet a numerically smaller German force but came up against an army more than twice its size. Nevertheless the German advance was temporarily held-up before retreat became the only option. The enemy then continued its rapid advance on Paris, the French and British in retreat. The Germans were stopped at the River Marne, a few miles to the east of the capital, at the beginning of September. Consider then, British soldiers had left England on August 12th, spent a few days becoming acclimatised and then as a cohesive fighting force moved by train up to the Belgium border. There they had fought a battle, in which to a large degree they had been successful, there were thousands of casualties on both sides. Then they retreated south west to the outskirts of Paris and made preparations for a serious counter attack. All this within three weeks, despite mostly marching.

So, at the Marne the French had assembled a new army to meet the German threat. It is probable that the highly successful German offensive was overstretched. With the BEF the French went on the offensive, surprising the Germans, and the Battle of the Marne resulted. Within a week or so the German army fell back about forty miles to the River Aisne, crossed it, taking up positions on the high ground, the Chemin des Dames ridge. There they dug trenches, sited machine guns, erected barbed wire, and from that time trench warfare began. What followed, was that as each side tried to outflank the other, more trenches were dug extending "the stalemate" situation across the whole countryside. So much for an early end to the war and it was not yet the end of September 1914.

In October the First Battle of Ypres was fought. This small town in Belgium became synonymous with the British army throughout the war. The German attack on Ypres was their last major strike of 1914, an attempt to overwhelm the British defences and sweep forward to Calais and the English Channel. However, Ypres, captured by the British at the beginning of October was to remain in Allied hands for the duration of the war. This epitomised the ability of a dedicated defender to hold back a determined attacker. The weapons of defence ruled. The British line held, and the seemingly unstoppable army that threatened to overrun Western Europe, was stopped.

At sea there had been two significant actions, the Battle of Coronel off Chile, where German commerce raiders on November 1st scored a victory over the Royal Navy's South American squadron. The armoured cruisers *Good Hope* and *Monmouth* were sunk without survivors. Cuckfield's Charles Randall and Charles Webber were serving on the Good Hope. A far larger and more powerful British fleet was dispatched to the Falkland Islands, where on December 8th British battlecruisers sank the German armoured cruisers *Scharnhorst* and *Gneisenau* as well as two more light cruisers. Several other ships escaped.

At home, income tax was doubled, the war was costing £1 million a day. By the end of the war that had multiplied eightfold.

In *Punch Magazine,* one writer prophetically forecast that the war would end at Christmas 1918.

As Christmas approached both sides rested, counted the casualties and made plans.

Both sides engaged in propaganda.

It was a time for reflection.

As 1915 began it became obvious that the war on the Western Front would not be fought as the combatants had expected just a few months previously.

It was not to be a fast flowing mobile war. At the beginning of the year the war was raging in many countries. The Eastern Fronts were delineated by fighting in Russia and Poland; the German Armies were therefore heavily engaged in the east and west. (The Schlieffen Plan, brilliantly conceived and responsible for the early successes, had effectively failed.)

> Schlieffen Plan - The German Army's plan for war against France and Russia. It was conceived by Count Alfred von Schlieffen as a direct response to the alliance between France and Russia in 1892. This was thought likely to compel Germany to fight its powerful neighbours in any future war. According to calculations, the general staff considered that in the event of war, France and Germany would be ready to fight a decisive battle within 15 days. Russia would not be ready for six weeks, by which time France would be beaten. The whole strategy was key to Germany's thinking up to 1914. The plan was to get round the French positions and strike at the rear. To achieve this it would be necessary to invade Belgium, by-passing the French fortress system, and sweep all aside before Britain could cross the channel. The French would be allowed to attack further south, the Germans tactically retreating, drawing in the French while their northern armies closed the trap. Had the original scheme been followed who knows what the outcome would have been. The German chief of staff, Molkte, maintained the essence of the plan. However, he reduced the number of troops through Belgium, preferring to reinforce the south. The Belgians showed unexpected resistance, the British Army arrived quicker than thought possible. The speed with which the Russian offensive in Prussia was mounted was a surprise, which meant that two German corps were transferred to the Eastern Front. But, Molkte's failure to maintain Schlieffen's concentration of forces in the north was crucial. The Battle of the Marne was the final blow to a technically brilliant plan not carried through. What followed was four years of attrition and waste.

The Austria-Hungary armies were mainly engaged in the east and in the Balkans. The Russians and Turks were fighting in the Caucasus and the British and the Turks in Mesopotamia. (This latter campaign by mainly Anglo-Indian troops). There were also campaigns in all four of Germany's African colonies. The ill-fated Gallipoli operation lasted from April 1915 until January 1916. It contained some of the worst conditions possible in which to carry out an offensive. Again, trench warfare predominated, sickness and disease were rife. The bravery of the troops and the role of the Anzac forces is legendary. It all started as an attempt to force a way through the Dardenelles to the Black Sea, inspired as a naval matter. It finished when, the new commander General Munroe and Kitchener the War Minister, visited the battlefront in November 1915 and ordered its evacuation.

All these peripheral campaigns, however dreadful to those fighting, remained secondary to the Western Front in terms of influencing the final outcome. Britain and Germany were the two largest industrialised powers in Europe. The full capacity of Britain's factories would be needed, ordnance and munitions in huge quantities. The tank had been conceived by the British at the end of 1914 and the first technical specification was finalised in June 1915. Prototypes were built and the tank was mass produced in 1916. The tank's purpose was to give support to the infantry when attacking trench strongholds. The Germans did not join the tank race, preferring to develop anti-tank weapons and strategy.

French attacks in the Champagne region from December 1914 to March 1915 had made little progress, but they suffered 90,000 casualties, (Plan 17 had failed).

> Plan 17 - The strategic plan for the wartime deployment of the French Army. The brainchild of General Foch and adopted by C in C Joffre, it was the blueprint for the invasion of Germany in response to the presumed attack on France. The plan was flexible without the rigid timetables of the Schlieffen Plan, scheduling a southern invasion of Lorraine and Alsace to the Rhine. The northern attack would carry the French through the Southern Ardennes. The French had manpower deficiences and also underestimated the German use of reserves to fill a defensive role. Plan 17 was put into action in August 1914, but, the Allied defeats at the Mons and the Battle of the Frontiers persuaded the French to withdraw.

It was 10th March 1915 before the first significant battle of the year for the British Army. The time had come to break through the German line of defence set up the previous autumn. The BEF launched its offensive at Neuve Chappelle in Artois, broke through, but was unable to secure a worthwhile bridgehead, for the loss of 13,000 casualties.

In April the German army launched a limited offensive at Ypres, it was their only major attack of 1915. The strategy was to try out a form of attack with limited objectives only, and importantly, introduce the German high command's new weapon, chlorine gas. It marked the first use of poison gas. There were huge losses on both sides and no real land changed hands. In May the Artois offensive took place. This was the French C in C, Joffre's second attempt at a major breakthrough. The French were supported by the British First Army around Neuve Chappelle. For eighteen days battles raged back and forth, costing the Germans 90,000 casualties, the French 100,000 and the British about 26,000.

It was during this battle that the infamous "shell scandal" was uncovered. The shortage of ammunition for British artillery caused the downfall of the Liberal Government. The Prime Minister, Mr Asquith, was forced to form a coalition government with the Conservatives. A new Ministry of Munitions under David Lloyd George was formed. This proved a resounding success.

"IF YOU KNOW OF A BETTER 'OLE ..."

The SS *Lusitania* was torpedoed and sunk off Ireland on May 7th. On May 31st London suffered its first zeppelin raid.

There were many other engagements in 1915, but the third and final "big push" that year came again from the Allies. The second Artois and Champagne campaigns, started on September 25th. The British and French armies took part in the Artois operations, using poison gas for the first time, the British attacking Loos and Lens, the French, Vimy Ridge. Results of six weeks fighting with attack and counter attack found the opposing armies almost in the same positions as at the start. Bad weather had the last word, causing the hostilities to end. The Allies lost about 100,000 casualties and the Germans half that number, emphasising the superiority of good defensive positions. The Champagne attack was no more success over all. The French pushed half a million men against the German defences. By November 6th, with casualties for this and the Artois expedition mounting to close on 300,000 it was time to take a winter break and recuperate.

How on earth could these losses go on? They could and they did! The campaigns of the Somme and Passchendaele weren't on the menu yet! – 1915 ended. Both sides were gassing each other, chemical warfare began.

The poem that follows was first written in October 1917, and reflects the poet's bitter views of the reality of war. It seems particularly appropriate introduced at this time, illuminating the dire consequences of the use of poison gas. Wilfred Owen suggests, Horace's famous line from Od., III. ii.13, *dulce et decorum est pro patria mori*. It is sweet and glorious to die for one's country – was a lie.

DULCE ET DECORUM EST – Wilfred Owen M.C.

Bent double, like old beggars under sacks,
Knock-kneed, coughing like hags, we cursed through sludge,
Till on the haunting flares we turned our backs
And towards our distant rest began to trudge.
Men marched asleep. Many had lost their boots
But limped on, blood-shod. All went lame; all blind;
Drunk with fatigue; deaf even to the hoots
Of tired, outstripped Five-Nines that dropped behind.

Gas! Gas! Quick, boys! – An ecstasy of fumbling,
Fitting the clumsy helmets just in time;
But someone still was yelling out and stumbling,
And flound'ring like a man in fire or lime . . .
Dim, through the misty panes and thick green light,
As a green sea, I saw him drowning.

In all my dreams, before my helpless sight,
He plunges at me, guttering, choking, drowning.

If in some smothering dreams you too could pace
Behind the wagon that we flung him in,
And watch the white eyes writhing in his face,
His hanging face like a devil's sick of sin;
If you could hear, at every jolt, the blood
Come gargling from the froth-corrupt lungs,
Obscene as cancer, bitter as the cud
Of vile, incurable sores on innocent tongues,-
My friend, you would not tell with such high zest
To children ardent for some desperate glory,
The old Lie: Dulce et decorum est
Pro patria mori.

GASSED
by John Singer Sargent

Nineteen sixteen began with a very important change to the British Government's strategy. Despite the number of casualties, to supply the rapidly expanding British Army, conscription laws were passed for the first time. The Military Services Act, 1916 became law in February. By the end of the war more than 2.3 million conscripts entered service.

Training camps had sprung up all over Britain, and the ever increasing army was in evidence everywhere. In 1916 it was recorded in Mid Sussex that the rainfall measured as falling on over two hundred days and the amount was 50% higher than the yearly average.

All these sketches were done during training. It really did rain in 1916.

The British sense of humour prevails.

Planners on both sides had very firm views of what was required to gain a supreme victory in 1916. The Germans chose the Battle of Verdun and the Allies, the Battle of the Somme. It is worth studying the thinking behind both, with the results.

First, Verdun. The German Chief of Staff, General Falkenhayn, believed that the way to gain a decisive victory was to bleed the French Army using a combination of military strategy and psychology. The theory was, that Verdun, having no really obvious military importance as a fortress, was however immensely prestigious to the French cause. Thus, it would be defended at all costs. (Psychology). Reasoning that the Russians and the British could not be knocked out with a single blow, Falkenhayn decided to grind the French into defeat by inflicting unsustainable casualties over a long offensive. A breakthrough was not on the agenda. The French would stay at Verdun until they would no longer be strong enough to continue in the war. (Military strategy). Verdun, reasonably close to the German railway network, was vulnerable to the concentration of unprecedented quantities of artillery and ammunition.

On February 21st the attack began, the Germans throwing in one million troops, France's defence force initially numbering 200,000. The first German artillery barrage used over one million shells. On February 27th superb French counter artillery tactics stopped the German advance and what followed was a series of battles that raged until December 1916. Verdun did not fall, the French army was hurt badly but so was the German. The war of attrition was successful in that records show that the French lost 550,000 men and the Germans 430,000. About half the casualties died!

Second, while this carnage was going on, further north, the Allies were planning their own decisive campaign, the Battle of the Somme! The brainchild of the French C in C Joffre and supported by General Haig the battle was, although aimed at territorial gain, an attempt to destroy German Manpower Reserves. With the German's mass assault at Verdun the planning of the Somme offensive devolved on General Haig. The build-up took months. Vast stocks of ammunition and stores of all kinds were accumulated within a convenient distance of the front. Miles of new railways and trench tramways were laid, and all available roads were improved. Scores of miles of trenches were dug with gun emplacements, observation posts and masses of telephone wires etc. There was no surprise awaiting the enemy. The German defence was probably the strongest of the whole war.

The battle was preceded by eight days of artillery bombardment. Nearly two years in preparation the defending troops nestled in deep bunkers awaiting the end of the artillery barrage.

The allied attack deployed 750,000 men in total over the campaign. When the British advanced, the Germans rose from their underground refuge virtually unscathed.

There were some initial gains, but that fateful day July 1st 1916, saw the British suffer more casualties than on any other day in the history of the

British army! There were many battles on the whole of the Somme salient. Attack and counter-attack took place over the weeks and months until November when the snows intervened. By which time the British had gained a few miles and suffered 420,000 casualties, the French 200,000 and the Germans maybe 500,000.

BEFORE THE BATTLE - Siegfried Sassoon, M.C. June 1916.

> Music of whispering trees
> Hushed by a broad-winged breeze
> Where shaken water gleams;
> And evening radiance falling
> With reedy bird-notes calling.
> O bear me safe through dark, you low-voiced streams.
>
> I have no need to pray
> That fear may pass away;
> I scorn the growl and rumble of the fight
> That summons me from cool
> Silence of marsh and pool
> And yellow lillies islanded in light.
> O river of stars and shadows, lead me through the night.

Thus taking Verdun and the Somme together, fighting started in February and finished in November. Little land changed hands and nearly two million men from both sides became casualties. Victory or defeat! Whose? The battle wrecked the BEF's new volunteer mass army.

While these huge war winning efforts were taking place Salonika, the Italian campaigns, Mesopotamia and the Balkan conflicts were raging. Romania declared war on the Central Powers and many other regional struggles were happening. All the place names and battle honours are well recorded in the varied and many history books written about the war.

The multitude of towns and villages fought over in the battle zones were all featured in the press reports at the time. Places unheard of by the vast majority of the British public then have become important features in the history of many of our regiments.

The month of May saw the only confrontation between the British Grand Fleet and the German High Seas Fleet, the world's two largest navies. As we have seen, the race to build the most powerful navy had contributed to the political instability of the pre-war period. Without knowing it both fleets were finally at sea at the same time, albeit with differing objectives. On the last day of the month 274 ships and some 70,000 seamen met in conflict at the Battle of Jutland. As for ships sunk it was a minor tactical success for the German fleet. Battleships, Battlecruisers, Cruisers and Destroyers fought over great distances from mid-afternoon until nightfall. Each navy tried to draw the other into what each believed to be a trap for the other. Three British Battlecruisers were literally blown to pieces, the German ships also suffered much damage. Finally the German navy retreated to port with their pyrrhic victory and left the British Grand Fleet supreme in the North Sea for the rest of the war.

Field Marshall Kitchener the War Minister, was killed on June 5th, when his transport to Russia, the Cruiser *Hampshire*, struck a mine off the Orkney Islands.

As 1916 drew to an end the war was in a desperate stalemate. Probably the war's attritive nature was responsible for the first signs of weakening of Germany's resources. At what cost? On December 12th in the Reichstag, German Chancellor, Bethmann Hollweg made a peace offer. Germany declared that it had been forced into war to exercise freedom of national development. It stressed that its troops were secure in occupied territory and called for the Allies to open talks because further fighting was futile. No mention was made of peace terms or reparations and guarantees already stipulated by the Allies. By the end of the month the offer had been rejected. The Germans had hoped for helpful participation from the American government, but without success. President Wilson's Peace Note of December 16th only served to highlight the differences between the warring countries. Germany answered this by adopting unrestricted submarine warfare, thus ensuring that American involvement was inevitable.

At home there was a crisis facing the government. By the end of the year the population had become war-weary. There was a need to reinforce the BEF. Food supply was being affected by the German submarine blockade. The military mistakes at Gallipoli, the Mesopotamia front and at Jutland together with the Irish problem (Easter rising), all contributed to a weakening of Prime Minister Asquith's position. The ultimate tactical failure of the Somme offensive was the final straw. The coalition collapsed on December 5th. David Lloyd George who had been Kitchener's successor in the summer, resigned. He was promptly invited to lead a new and stronger coalition, becoming the Prime Minister on December 7th. So, 1916 ended ...

THE MARCH-PAST - Siegfried Sassoon, M.C. 25 December 1916

In red and gold ribbon the Corps-Commander stood,
With ribboned chest puffed out for all to see:
He'd sworn to beat the Germans, if he could;
For God had taught him strength and strategy.
He was our leader, and a judge of Port –
Rode well to hounds, and was a damned good sort.

"Eyes right!" We passed him with a jaunty stare,
"Eyes front!" He'd watched his trusted legions go.
I wonder if he guessed how many there
Would get knocked out of time in next week's show.
"Eyes right!" The corps-commander was a Mute;
And Death leered round him, taking our salute.

2

JANUARY - MARCH 1917
The Scene Continued
– At Home

What of Cuckfield in 1917? It was a small town like so many others in rural England, with a large number of its men away at the war. It was no longer called a market town in the trade directories. In 1917 it was known as a union town and parish, pleasantly situated on an eminence in the centre of the county of Sussex. Within the diocese of Chichester, Cuckfield was in the rural deanery of Cuckfield and the archdeaconary of Lewes. For civil jurisdiction it was in the Haywards Heath petty sessional division and county court district; the Cuckfield division and county court having merged with Haywards Heath in 1897.

The last ten-yearly census carried out in 1911 revealed that the population of Cuckfield was 1,879 on the civil register, and 2,678 in the ecclesiastical parish. Part of the parish was ceded to St Wilfred's of Haywards Heath in May 1911, by order of the Church Council. Cuckfield's position within the Rural Deanery can be measured by its contribution to the Bishop of Winchester's Fund. Of the sixteen parishes concerned, its levy was 17% of the total compared to Haywards Heath's 12%, Lindfield's 8.5% and Crawley's 8%.

There were four places to worship. The parish church, the Holy Trinity had 600 sittings. The Congregational chapel in Broad Street had 190 sittings. The Baptist chapel in Polestub had 100 sittings and there was the Wesleyan chapel at Whiteman's Green. In addition there were the Mission rooms, St. John's in Ansty and All Saints in Brook Street. Both these were administered by the parish church. The number of sittings suggests an indication of the relative strengths of the parish church, Church of England, and the Nonconformist community. Important roles played by the two main churches were as rallying points for the townsfolk seeking comfort and information. The clergy performed its spiritual function and adopted the guise of war commentator with the necessary jingoism to maintain a high level of morale and patriotism.

By 1917 the clubs and societies listed at the outbreak of the war had sadly diminished. Lack of active membership of the sports clubs was obvious with the younger men away. The football, cricket and athletic clubs had no entries in *Kelly's* directory of the time. The vast majority of the young, and sometimes the not so young had left. In the four years of the war over 400 men served with the armed services, eighty-one did not return.

There were thirty or so shops in Cuckfield, from clothing to food, from watchmaking to stationery. There was the main post office in the High Street and sub offices in Broad Street, Ansty and Whiteman's Green. Mail arrived and was despatched at least three times a day. Whiteman's Green itself had sufficient shops to meet the basic needs and was a shopping destination for folk from Brook Street and Staplefield. The town had its own Gas Works, a company over fifty years old. It was supplied with water from the works at Balcombe, the property of the Mid Sussex Water Board, representing the Urban District Councils of Cuckfield Rural, Cuckfield Urban and Haywards Heath (remember the takeover battle of 1897). A motor bus service was in operation; it passed through Cuckfield three times a day from Brighton to Lindfield. Housing development had taken place in London Lane, Broad Street, London Road and Courtmead Road.

The Queen's Hall was listed together with its library as a public establishment and was the meeting place of the Cuckfield Urban District Council. During the war it had become a VAD hospital. At Cuckfield Park there was a War Hospital Supply Depot staffed by volunteer women who worked long hours. Many other voluntary organisations prospered. The all important role now demanded of women; still, without suffrage, grew daily.

Most of the town's roads were tarred. The District Council employed a surveyor who was responsible for the town's infrastructure. Included in his staff were two full-time road maintenance workers. Each year many tons of tar, sand and granite chippings were used to repair the surface of Cuckfield's roads, from Mill Hall cottages and part way towards Brook Street, to South Street and Broad Street to Haywards Heath. In addition to this continuing work all other road and footpath repairs were attended to. The surveyor's job was a very demanding one, each month he submitted a hand written report to the District Council. Other employees looked after the council's land, sewage works etc.

The streets lit by gas, at night there was a blackout curfew with severe punishment if broken. There was no radio, let alone television, war news with a degree of propaganda was supplied by the newspapers for those that took them. People mainly walked, some had cycles, there were a few cars and lorries. Horses and carts were still much used, but when the Council's horse died in July, a replacement was impossible due to war requirements.

The townsfolk attended the many meetings called to further the war effort. Entertainment was mainly locally inspired as always. Concerts performed by friends and neighbours and the patients at the VAD Hospital were very popular. There was a cinema in Haywards Heath, and for some, theatres in Brighton.

The 'workhouse' in Ardingly Road continued as ever to play an important role in the affairs of the district. In 1913 its title was officially changed to a Poor Law Institution and it became known as West Hylands. It was through the Poor Law Amendment Act of 1834 that a "union of parishes" was derived, the Poor Law Commissioners actively encouraging or coercing parishes to form unions in order to make large workhouse buildings viable.

The towns and villages making up the Cuckfield Union, excluding Haywards Heath and Cuckfield itself, made up the Cuckfield Rural District Council. Their meeting place and office were in Boltro Road, Haywards Heath.

In 1907 the Church of England School, the National School, absorbed the pupils from the British School at the Congregational Church. The schools amalgamated under the County Council's education authority. There was a girl's boarding school at Warden Court.

Cuckfield was a very strong farming community and the farms worked to a high level of production. There were twenty-five farms listed in *Kelly's Directory* in 1917. In addition to wheat and oats there were dairy and beef cattle. Pig breeding was encouraged as was the use of land for allotments.

On December 26th 1916 in the *Mid Sussex Times*, the local newspaper, there was written a small piece, not attributed to any correspondent and entitled, "Its bit":

> Farther north I perceive another grey spire in the historic little town of Cuckfield. In and around that grand old church are many reminders of bygone times. The Reverend Sylvester Home MP was born there or thereabouts and Henry Kingsley lies sleeping. To the right with its water tower is the Haywards Heath asylum. Old Gypsy Lee the far famed fortune teller at the Dyke died there at the age of seventy. Dickens left his historic mark on Lindfield and Nelson on Slaugham. All together Mid Sussex has done and is doing "its bit" in Ancient and Modern History.

So, having set the scene with a summary of the war so far, and updating the civil information on the town, read on . . .

On January 2nd the *Mid Sussex Times* published the list of those killed in the district since the outbreak of war. Every week this list was a feature in the paper, each new death recorded, and then repeated the next week. The victims' families must have found this very traumatic. In that first edition of 1917, Cuckfield's tally was thirty-seven.

Life was very sombre. As described, the war was in stalemate. The newspapers portrayed the action overseas in as much detail as possible, censorship allowing. The *Mid Sussex Times*, devoted several columns to the description of the fighting on all fronts. Of course national papers were available but, in 1917, many people in rural areas would have relied upon their "locals". On other pages much space was used to encourage the civilian population of the towns and villages to make more and more effort to be useful to their country. The leader articles pleaded for patriotism, reduction of waste and more food production; and generally reminding all with the constant theme that the country was threatened. It was everybody's duty to do something about it!

In the *Mid Sussex Times* of January 9th:

In pre-war days a patriot was someone who bawled jingo choruses at a smoking concert or music hall. But that is all changed: a patriot of today is one who either fights for his country or works for his country. No one else counts. There are a great many patriots in England but there could be more! The statements made at Local Tribunals as to "sheltering" make the blood boil of patriots who hold that the welfare of the country should stand before anything and everything. The question put at Tribunals - "Where would your business be if we couldn't get men for the Army?", we have never heard a satisfactory answer. The reason is obvious. It is only by keeping up the strength of our fighting forces that the enemy can be kept from our shores. Once the Germans landed, businesses and homes would collapse like a pack of cards. Have you realised that? Ponder over the facts for a few moments, and then, perhaps, you will not say hard things of the Military Representatives and Tribunals for hardening their hearts. They know their duty if you do not yours.

The traders of Cuckfield decided that from New Year's Day they would adopt "dinner hour" closing between 1pm and 2pm. The Ship Inn slate club having completed its 22nd year in 1916 started a new year with Mr W T Fox as its secretary. Eighty members were pleased to carry on this method of receiving a small payment when sick, and also saving for Christmas.

On New Year's day Mrs Murrell of Braines Mead heard that her son George was not "missing" but a prisoner of war in Germany.

The Urban District Council met on January 4th. The members were Mr R Anscombe, chairman, Miss E Payne, Messrs S Knight, T I Symons, J Denman, S Caffyn, B Burtenshaw, A Beeching, E Napper, H Bates, C H Waugh (Clerk) and A Croucher (Surveyor). A letter from the East Sussex War Agricultural Committee enquired about what steps the Council had taken to increase the growth of potatoes. The Council resolved to offer its own land in Glebe field, for allotments, before dealing with any other land. Mr Beeching offered land of his near Blunt's Wood for potato growing, free of charge, on the applicant paying the rates. A committee comprising, Messrs Anscombe, Knight and Beeching, was appointed to deal with allotments under the new scheme. It was resolved to inform the War Agricultural Committee, the Council was prepared to give ten rood allotments free for one year and provide seed potatoes at cost. Tamplin's Brewery was given permission to make a small channel along the footpath by the King's Head. The Surveyor's application for a war bonus was refused. He was awarded an extra ten shillings per month for looking after the Council's horse.

The motor bus now ran from Cuckfield to Haywards Heath. The horse drawn omnibus, linking the town with the railway station, had given excellent service over many years. As from New Year's day the Brighton Line's train, the *Southern Belle* would cease to run, it would be a temporary measure until the end of the war. For eight years these magnificent trains composed entirely of Pullman cars and drawn by one of the company's most powerful engines had been a familiar sight . . . *"a streak of light, during the journey from Brighton to London in one hour, and returning on the same day. In peacetime there was no more vivid a picture of London life at its gayest and brightest as the well-dressed crowd that buzzed about on the Southern Belle prior to its departure. Of late the crowd has been tinged with khaki and blue."* The train, was first built and brought into service in November 1908. There had been advances in carriage construction during the intervening years, but the original design was still considered superior. It was announced, that, the remaining Pullman service, would cease until the end of the war. The fares would be increased to 1s 6d first class, and 1s 0d third class, instead of 1s 0d and 9d.

The Urban District of Cuckfield and the Cuckfield Rural District Council had their own local Tribunals in common with other districts such as Haywards Heath and Burgess Hill. What is a Tribunal? A dictionary may describe it as a "Court of Justice". In the article on page 24 from the *Mid Sussex Times*, and, as in further chapters, the tribunal was indeed similar to a court. It was convened solely to decide a man's right to be exempt from going to war. Tribunals came into being following the introduction of the Military Services Act 1916, when conscription became law.

> Military Services Act, 1916. The first conscription laws ever passed in Great Britain. It was in response to the rapid growth of the Army and the necessary expansion of the munitions industry. The first bill involved the calling-up of single men and childless widowers aged 18 to 41, starting with those who had already attested willingness to serve, under Lord Derby's voluntary registration scheme of 1915. Clergymen, vital war workers and conscientious objectors were exempt. Absolutist objectors who refused alternative non-combatant duties were rarely granted exemption by local tribunals. Lord Derby, opposed to conscription, was the Director of Recruitment in 1915. Seeking an alternative to conscription he asked all eligible males for voluntary assent to service if called upon, promising that married men would be called last. However, the scheme provided less than 350,000 potential troops and was abandoned in December 1915. Unfamiliarity with the conscription process soon showed. Married attestees began to receive call-up papers during March 1917 before many unattested bachelors, prompting a revised second act in May. British conscription radically expanded during the crisis on the Western Front in the spring of 1918. A new act was passed in April of that year calling up 51 year olds. By the end of the war more than 2.3 million conscripts entered military service.

Tribunal members comprised local dignitaries, District Councillors, one member representing the military. In Cuckfield's case, Mr B Y Bevan, a Second Lieutenant in the Volunteers fulfilled that task. The clerk to the tribunal was Mr C H Waugh, the Council's clerk. The chairman was Mr Edwin Mumford Preston of Cuckfield Park. Vicar Canon Wilson sometimes attended

On Boxing Day 1916 at the Queen's Hall, a case was heard, by which a butcher applied for his slaughterman, the only one left in the parish, to be exempt from service. The man was in the volunteers and drilled regularly, it was decided to give him exemption until the end of March 1917, subject to a substitute being found. The manager of Cuckfield Gas Works made a further plea speaking for a stoker. The tribunal clerk had been in communication with the Ministry of Munitions. He had received a letter, stating it would be necessary for the gas works to have sufficient labour to carry out an efficient operation. It did not appear that the company had any surplus labour now; on the other hand the stoker was clearly a man who should be serving in the army if possible. The verdict, that the stoker was granted further exemption, until a substitute could be found.

All tribunals' meetings were reported in the press, but the names of the appellants and sponsors were withheld. A solicitor's name who represented an appellant, was published. There was obvious bitterness in small communities where exemption from military service was concerned. Some more of the proceedings are below.

The Cuckfield Rural District Council Tribunal met early in January. Their members, were District Councillors, the chairman, Major Lister also having that role with the tribunal. The clerk was Mr C H Waugh, Mr F McClaren the military representative and Mr W Wood represented the Board of Agriculture. A Cuckfield farmer and carter, in partnership with two brothers farmed 136 acres. His application for exemption had been previously adjourned awaiting a medical examination, produced a certificate for B1 service. He had joined the Volunteers as requested and had made himself efficient. Mr Wood supported the application, farming an important occupation, conditional exemption was granted.

There does seem to have been a variety of people seeking exemption from call-up and no doubt there were some malingerers among the worthy applicants. But, the so-called experts who decided the cases certainly wielded enormous power. It must have been a very daunting experience attending a tribunal knowing that the first consideration was to fill the army. There were many definite reserved occupations, it wasn't until May 1918 that all males up to 51 years of age were called-up. Desperation. A few more examples follow, just to give the reader a feel for this incredibly difficult period in our history.

A Lindfield resident applied on behalf of his gardener aged 41, who had charge of 16 acres and a drainage system. He had been passed for C1 service and that only an able-bodied man could do his work. Exemption was granted. A Hurstpierpoint watchmaker aged 32, whose case had been adjourned to enable him to obtain munitions work, had been passed for C1 service. The case was further adjourned for another three months to allow the applicant to join the Munitions Volunteer Reserve.

A really interesting case emerged concerning a Keymer orchid grower. He had been passed for general service, but, nevertheless had applied for a continuation of his exemption. He had devoted his life to orchid growing. Represented by Mr F Donne, a solicitor, it was said that if called-up, thousands of pounds worth of stock would be lost. The chairman asked whether orchid growing was of national importance. Mr Donne said that it was of national importance not to destroy all this capital, and if this man was taken the business would close down. One month's final exemption was granted.

A Bolney widow applied for an extension for her son, a carpenter and farm foreman, who had worked for her since his father's death. Mr Wood, the Board of Agriculture's representative, claimed to have known this farm for 45 years. He said that it would be impossible for anybody to produce more from its 33 acres. The widow being over seventy years of age could not handle the work. One month's final exemption was granted!!

And finally at this point, the Cuckfield Urban Tribunal heard a case of a bus driver, 29 years old, no longer employed by his company, due to the company temporarily closing down its operation He had, however, possible alternate employment with Brighton Buses until his own bus company restarted. With the increase in railway fares this was likely. His category was for C1 service, a low one. He was now suffering from arthritis and did not think he would be fit for military service. One member of the Tribunal remarked *"that some people had been known to put on flesh at it"*, the applicant said that he had been trying to put on flesh for 20 years without success. The clerk, amid laughter, said *"You'd better see what the army can do for you"*. Probably in desperation the bus driver then said that he was trying to get work as a driver in a gunpowder factory. He was granted exemption for 14 days, final.

The importance of the tribunal system cannot be over emphasised, decisions were good and bad, there were certainly many, many cases where the potential servicemen were less than A1. Perhaps this was expected.

 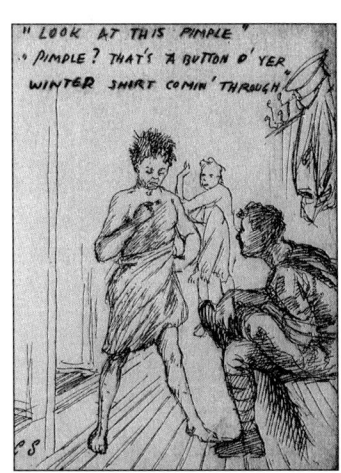

A little light relief from Geoffrey Squire.

Mr Richard Worsley who had died in November 1916, at the age of eighty, left the considerable sum of £491,510. He had been a director of Whitbread and Co. (Brewers) Ltd.

Entertainment in such dour times was of paramount importance. Those living in bigger towns and cities still had a good choice of events to see. Sailors and soldiers home on leave mingled with the civilian population to visit the theatres and of course places like London had much to offer. Zeppelin raids had featured as a spectacle, not least for their novelty. The nearest centre to Cuckfield for a variety of entertainment was Brighton. A typical week in early February featured, *"Peter Pan"* at the Theatre Royal, *"Mrs Gorringe's Necklace"* at the West Pier, *"Saphyr"* at the Palace Pier and for the cinema, *"The Dumb Genius"* and *"The Girl Who Loves a Soldier"* at the Palladium. For the people of Cuckfield, there was the Picture Theatre in Haywards Heath. It was sited in the Broadway and was reached either, by the motor bus, or more probably by walking. A classic programme would comprise more than one film, a serial and Pathe Gazette news. The *Mid Sussex Times* wrote:

> Of all the films the one that pleased and caused the heartiest laughter was one called, "Charlie the Perfect Lady". There is no need to say who Charlie was. There is only one Charlie to lovers of the movies, at times his attire was not that of a perfect lady, that was his misfortune but he made the most of it. As a mimic Charlie has few equals, he knows all the tricks of the fair sex. The sly manner, the glance of the amorous eye, the gentle swaying of the body and the shoulder shrugs which require but little effort but which mean so much. The girls simply roared over Charlie so true was he to life, the ladies of maturing years laughed as well. It was an understanding sort of laugh. The men wise in their generation swelled the laughter chorus and for the time being everybody was merry.

On February 13th at the Picture Theatre, the programme was; Charlie Chaplin in *"Charlie's Shanghaied"*, another comedy *"By Stork Delivery"*, Pathe's Gazette newsreel and the serial, episode 23 of the *"Diamond's in the Sky"* entitled *"The Double Cross"*.

There was a concert at the Drill Hall, in aid of the VAD Hospital. This hospital was housed in the Queen's Hall, therefore the need to hold the concert in the Drill Hall, the Queen's Hall's immediate predecessor. The organisers were Miss L M Gibb and Mr A T Rapley who announced that £9.12s had been given to the hospital. The entertainers were mostly local performers. Notably, Mr T Attewell who sang several pieces including *"The Yeoman's Wedding Song"* and *"Long Ago in Alcala"*. Miss Winifred Cleare played the piano and violin and accompanied other singers. A Mr Hugh Inman of Brighton, who sang at camp concerts and Red Cross hospitals every week, gave his services free of charge. His voice, a well-known tenor was a very popular attraction. Mr Attewell, a music teacher, was the organist at the Holy Trinity Church, a position he had held for over twenty years.

A Valentine's Day Dance with a whist drive was held at the Co-Operative Hall, Haywards Heath on February 14th. It was another case of finding an alternate venue to the Queen's Hall. A Jumble Sale at the Parish Room in aid of the Nursing Association was a big success.

The Picture Theatre advertised a big feature film, *"The Battle of the Ancre and the Advance of the Tanks"*. The publicity declared . . .

The Tanks have seized hold of the public imagination as nothing else in the war has done. You will see them just as our soldiers first saw them on the memorable morning last autumn, when those huge steel-clad monsters, impervious to everything but a direct hit from a shell, spread terror and death in the German ranks. More vivid battle scenes have never been shown on the screen. There is no suggestion of "fake", reality is stamped on every scene. When you see those appalling seas of mud you wonder how our gallant lads could ever have advanced at all, and the realisation fills you with new admiration for their achievement. The terrific fire of the British artillery is shewn. No wonder the Germans were nerve-shattered by the ordeal of such a bombardment. You see our brave boys dashing across "no man's land" on the way to victory. Later you see the bringing in of the wounded – the pitiful aftermath of the battle - and nothing could bring home to us more poignantly the noble sacrifices which our men are making for us . . .

> The Battle of Ancre was the last British attack in the Somme offensive. It was the BEF's one last effort on the far east of the salient on November 13th 1916. Beaumont Hamel was captured. The first snows of winter halted the campaign. The Mark 1 tank entered service in June 1916, just in time to be available for the Somme, but its debut during the offensive was considered an anti climax.
>
> By September 15th there were forty-nine Mk 1 tanks ready for the Battle of Flers-Courcelette. Thirty-two took part, but, apparently at the expense of under trained men and under tested vehicles. A tank's perfomance, six miles an hour maximum, but was more likely three. This, combined with shell holes and dreadful mud, often meant that the infantry arrived first. Many tanks broke down. Their marginal success, some said relative failure, was greeted with enthusiasm by the British press and indeed by Field Marshall Haig. The tank made a bigger contribution when the Mark IV became available in the middle of 1917. It clearly created a huge propaganda initiative.
>
> The Germans eventually designed and produced a tank, the AV7 Panzerkampfwagen. It was the heaviest, fastest and best armed machine used by either side. It was also cumbersome and an easy target. Due to the cost only a handful of units were produced.

The government was urgently seeking ways of financing the war. Early in 1917 two distinct schemes were in being, a government war loan paying 5% interest, and national savings certificates. In January Cuckfield decided to have its own War Savings Association. A meeting was convened in the Parish

Room. Mr E M Preston voted Chairman and Treasurer and Miss Turner the Secretary. The committee comprised Mrs Cleare and Messrs Vaughan, Herrington, Napper, Funnell and Green. The scheme adopted was of subscribing 6d per week, for the purchase of War Savings Certificates. An individual saving 6d a week for 31 weeks would purchase a certificate for 15s 6d redeemable in five years for £1.00d. Within three weeks the Association had two hundred members, and purchased 500 certificates.

On February 17th Cuckfield Urban District Council held a special meeting to approve an investment in the new 5% War Loan. From its own reserves it allocated £1,300. For the Haywards Heath Council to make an investment, it was necessary for them to borrow £500 from their bank. This does show the relative positions of the two towns in 1917. This 5% Loan actually raised one billion pounds. In *Punch*, came the anecdote, *"we love anagrams, the Chancellor of the Exchequer, Bonar Law's name rearranged, – War Loan B."*

In Cuckfield there were four churches. The largest was the parish church, the Holy Trinity. The next largest was the Congregational Church in Broad Street. A very significant number of Cuckfield families worshipped there. So when a meeting was arranged by the Burgess Hill Congregational Church, sponsoring an evening with the Salvation Army, an invitation was sent to Cuckfield. Staff Captain Littlejohn addressed a very large gathering, the subject, prospects of emigration to the Dominions for war widows. The idea was for them to settle in Canada, Australia or New Zealand after the war. The scheme allowed for "worthy" widows living in an unsatisfactory environment after the war to be given another chance. This idea tried in the past was a way of helping those without husbands after the war to resettle. Also, the host country benefited. It was felt that the Salvation Army, was well equipped to carry out this work. Whereas, the state, had no system to alleviate the hardships caused to widows and their children. It was an important aim to keep widows out of the workhouse. The meeting then heard from a Mr Chisholm, a Burgess Hill man, who praised the Salvation Army for its forward planning. He abhorred the state's apparent abdication of its responsibilities. Britain, he said, should solve these problems, not a voluntary organisation. The state has yet to learn that as a Christian state it had a Christian duty to its own people. Readers are left to form their own opinion of this, compulsory migration was an old cure, not universally liked but it solved a multitude of problems.

At the annual meeting in Brighton of the Sussex Congregational Union, of which Mr W Stevens JP of Cuckfield was the Hon Treasurer, it was stated that *"not a few "Sons of the Manse" are serving with the colours, the churches have been depleted of their young manhood, and Free Church Ministers are doing YMCA work in France and taking service in the military camps."* The Reverend S Maddock, Cuckfield's Congregational Minister, who, at this meeting was elected as next year's President, was one of those serving in France. He worked with the YMCA for three months from early January. After two and a half weeks he sent a letter from Flanders to Mrs Cleare for her to let the people of Cuckfield know how he was getting on.

> Dear Mrs Cleare, - It is now two and a half weeks since I arrived here, and I feel that the friends of Cuckfield will be interested in some account of what I have seen and how I have been spending my time. After a fairly rough but uneventful crossing, we arrrived at the French port and were met by the YMCA car. This car meets every boat, and if there are friends of wounded on board they are first of all seen to, and carried by car to the hospital where their friends are - it may be 50 or 60 miles away - left there, brought back again, housed, fed if needful for the time being, and then safely dispatched home. A night or two ago the hospitality of the YMCA Headquarters was taxed to the extent of accommodating 12 newly arrived workers and 25 friends of the wounded . . . (Reverend Maddock worked in a YMCA "hut" not far from the trenches) . . . "I don't know what we should do without it," said a driver at about 2am one morning. A private came to me yesterday morning and handing me a ten franc note said, "Will you accept it as an appreciation of the noble work you are doing here for us?" I like night duty – and more than half my work here has been night duty – because it gives one chances of talking with the men. It is an experience worth coming out for. Every night a number of men and officers come from the lines to wait for trains or to report to various officers in the morning, and spend the night in the hut. We have frequently between 80 and 90, and it is a weird sight to walk among their prone forms on the floor in the darkened hut . . . In the middle of the hut is a stove, and that stove will be a memory of my life. A group of men always sit round it, and talk; and the talk of the men there would delight a newspaper correspondent, as the men compare notes of their trench experience, how they peered into the darkness on sentry duty till they could see "the trees forming fours"; stories of bombing raids, and shell holes, of trench hardships, of wounds and strafes, and hospitals and dugouts; of Fritz and Tommy, and their tricks and humours and forebearances. Then perhaps I must get on because a lorry has just arrived . . . (The Rev Maddock was another brave churchman, working within range of German guns),"selling cakes by the thousand and cocoa by the gallon". He came home in April.

On Sunday February 16th there was a memorial service at Cuckfield Parish Church. This was the fifth such service held since the war began. It was especially to honour those who had died since the last memorial service, Hubert Cartner, Frederick Divall, Ernest Henley, Albert Keep, Edward Lyon, Percival Morfee, Frank Rowland, Victor Denyer. The patriotism of the time shone through, as did an element of jingoism in Canon Wilson's address. It was obviously essential to maintain the morale of everyone. He chose as his sermon Acts 21, verse 39. He referred to Paul telling his captors that he, Paul, was "a citizen of no mean city, and I beseech thee, suffer me to speak unto the people". Canon Wilson applied those words to the situation of the day. *"We too could say that they were citizens of no mean city, they were members of the greatest empire the world had ever seen, but remember that greatness of an empire consisted not of its extent but in its men."* He went on to say that men had given their lives on the seas, in Flanders, in France, Salonika and Gallipoli, Egypt and Mesopotamia and Africa. It had been a wonderful display of self sacrifice, courage, endurance and cheerfulness in spite of the most awful trials. He very feelingly referred to Cuckfield's losses over the last two and a half years. Those who had given their lives were well known, and in honouring their memory they thanked God. By their self sacrifice they had shown they were citizens of no mean city. Then came the morale boosting. The *Mid Sussex Times* reported the vicar, as saying:

> Our enemies were making one last desperate thrust and had substituted a policy of ruthless savagery with a view to bringing wanton suffering to this land of ours. Hitherto we could almost say the war had hardly touched us. We had not felt the horror of it in the way that France, Belgium and Serbia had done but we should feel it in the days to come, there was no doubt about this. This war would be won, not only by the valour of our men and the supply of munitions, but by the supply of money, the country that had the last million of money would win the war. How essential is it therefore, that they would support the great war loan. Economy was also necessary today more than ever, and all should try and live according to the scale laid down by the Government. It might not be found an easy matter. Think of the number of ships that had been sunk and the cargoes of feeding stuffs that had been destroyed by enemy submarines! All should understand that there was a greater need of self denial in the future if we were going to win the war. It was not a question of could we afford to pay: it was not a question of pocket, but of patriotism. There should be less thought of self and more for others and of our country. Rich and poor alike should bear that in mind. The future might hold for us an enormous amount of suffering, therefore let us steel our hearts and bear with fortitude whatever trials, difficulties and sorrows that may come upon us, and shew ourselves worthy of these brave men who have given their lives for us and worthy to win victory.

A large part of Canon Wilson's address has been included in this narrative so that the gravity of the time in early 1917 can be appreciated. How else could the ordinary citizen of a small rural town be exhorted to greater effort? There was no television or radio. The country could not be bound together by its elected leaders other than by newspapers, or perhaps word of mouth. Therefore it seems logical that a prominent and respected member of the community should take up the mantle of "cheerleader". Who better than the local vicar? Where better than at church with its captive audience? It is therefore easy to believe the hardening of resolve that this type of address could accomplish.

Let us turn to a totally different subject. In 1917, most of the homes in Cuckfield were rented. In spite of the war, domestic business had to flourish, and none more so than the local building society. The Haywards Heath

Building Society held its AGM on February 26th and included amongst its Directors from Cuckfield, was Reuben Anscombe and Charles Waugh. The report said that the society was in good health. There was £50,000 out in mortgages and the reserve fund stood at £3,543. For savers, 4% interest was offered. There were 140 mortgages now held by the society. About 100 were on average less than £250, proving that the society was keeping its pledge to bring home ownership to those with lower incomes. The interest to savers of 4% was free from income tax, then at 25%.

It seems strange to think that there were such stringent restrictions, about the showing of lights, during the hours of darkness. Air warfare had more or less been restricted to regions of infantry fighting. Zeppelins had first made their appearance over England in 1915, but there were no long range bombers then. All this changed when the modified Gotha G-V began attacks on England in June. On the 27th Margate & Broadstairs were bombed. The showing of lights was a punishable offence.

In the Haywards Heath Magistrates' Court in February there were cases brought by the Cuckfield Police in respect of blackout infringements. Two cases concerned the Workhouse, both reported by Sergeant Potter. He said he noticed them while he was walking from Balcombe to Cuckfield, at 5.25pm on January 31st. He had noticed bright lights burning, coming from the building, shining in a northerly direction that he could see a quarter of a mile away. The first concerned Nurse McClare, in charge of the maternity unit, who said she was responsible but it was probably a patient who turned up the gas. Nurse McClare was fined ten shillings. The second concerned the head nurse, Miss George. The lights were shining from the Nurses' Home. Blinds were fitted but not drawn. The defendant said that the lights had been left burning to keep the water pipes from freezing. It was the maids day off, and closing the blinds was forgotten. She was fined ten shillings.

A third case was against Minnie Bartley, a maid at Leyton House (Cuckfield House), accused of showing a light through the fanlight over the front door. The maid, not the owner, was held fully responsible. Perhaps she was away from home. A little strange, particularly as the fine was quite severe compared with above, poor Minnie's penalty was £1. The *Mid Sussex Time's* headline over this one said: "A Bright Half Moon Over Cuckfield" (The fanlight is still there).

A happier note, Sergeant Ernest Attwater married Miss Alice Ethel Hulls at the Arundel Parish Church. The bridegroom was a well-known local athlete and before the outbreak of war was a professional cricketer with Surrey. The bride was the only daughter of Mr and Mrs Hulls of Arundel. Her father was a former Mayor of Arundel. Ernest went to France with the Royal Sussex Regiment on September 1st 1915 and took part in the Loos, Ypres and Somme campaigns. He was in England at this time training for a commission. It was offered to him in recognition of his meritorious service. He was a member of the Machine Gun Corps.

On March 6th there was an increase in price of the *Mid Sussex Times*, from 1d to 1 1/2d, the first increase since its inception in 1881.

On March 10th an important meeting took place in the Parish Room. It concerned the new National Service movement, put in place by the Government to encourage everybody to take part in the nation's work force. The Reverend Canon Wilson chaired the meeting and introduced the assembly to Major Kerney-Herbert of Hillbrow, Cuckfield, recently appointed Travelling Agent for the South East District - National Service. He addressed the meeting: *"Work, not shrink is the Battlecry. It is our bounden duty to put ourselves forward in any way we can to supply any deficiencies of labour that may be found to exist."* The scheme was voluntary. Men and women could enrol using a form from the Post Office, to do work for which they were best suited. Then the government could direct men and women to places of work in need of staff. It was voluntary and employees and employers would have the right of appeal. Members of the public asked questions. They were assured that those who volunteered for service, would not be moved unnecessarily, from their occupation or home. Besides volunteers for national service, canvassers, to call door to door recruiting likely candidates were needed.

The International Stores, who claimed to be the biggest grocers in the world, had a store in Cuckfield High Street (Where Penfolds is now). Once the National Service scheme got under way they included in their adverts the logo, "National Service Enrol Today, and relieve a fit man for the army."

News came, that Second Lieutenant Gunson, Royal Berkshire Regt, had been severely wounded in the thigh by a bomb. Before joining-up he was Mr Waugh's managing clerk.

Mrs Emma Knott, the oldest member of the Congregational Church died on March 17th at her home, Knowle Lodge. She was 88 years old and came to live in Cuckfield in 1852 with her parent's Mr and Mrs W Payne. The Payne family was deeply involved with the Public Hall and Free Library project in 1897; Miss Edith Payne was a District Councillor and the Librarian. The service, was held in the Chapel in the graveyard (Nonconformist). The close family, Mr Ernest Payne (nephew), Miss Edith Payne, Miss Amelia Payne, Mrs Dranefield (nieces), Mrs Cleare, Miss Ellen Payne, Miss Cleare (cousins), Mrs Ernest Payne and Miss Pratt were present. Mrs Knott was a tireless worker on Church affairs. She was heavily involved in the formation of the British School; all Sunday School matters, and she supported all improvements associated with the town. She was very popular.

An idea for a rather unique war memorial was conceived earlier in the year by Mr R A Bevan helped by Mr T W Best, which came to fruition in March. Both these gentlemen had worked tirelessly for Cuckfield over many years, and Mr Bevan in 1917 was in his twilight. He would be remembered as one of the principal characters behind the building of the Queen's Hall. The memorial consisted of a large frame, housing twenty-five photographs of Cuckfield men who died in the war. Beneath each photograph were their names, whether they were sailors or soldiers, and the date and place of death. The intention was to add to the memorial more photographs of the Queen's Hall. (Interestingly, this work can be seen today in the Cuckfield Museum).

Such was the interest in food conservation and production that every available opportunity was seized to contribute to the cause. In January the Urban District Council made allotments available. In March the Cuckfield Burial Board gave free use to the Managers of the School a plot of land near the Church. It was for the boys of the school to produce *"potatoes and other vegetables"*. The Headmaster, Mr W Herrington and Mr A Rapley, a teacher, supervised the work. The food problem was becoming critical. The U-Boat campaign was at its height and Britain's reliance on imports was being severely tested. In February the Prime Minister appealed to the nation in the House of Commons to observe a "National Lent". He called for sacrifice, saying that the nation would be better and stronger for it, both mentally and physically; accept the Food Controller's restrictions with voluntary food rationing. A suggested weekly ration of meat, bread and sugar was published.

VOLUNTARY RATIONING
The Food Controller's Appeal to the Nation

The necessity for some curtailment of the Nation's food consumption is urgent. An amount sufficient for each individual requires, in consequence to be stated. The quantity indicated as being sufficient has been arrived at on no haphazard basis, but after full examination of the actual position of stocks immediately available or visible. Only by the adoption of and working to such an average apportionment will it be possible to maintain an adequate margin to meet not only the actual situation but contingencies which are to be allowed for. The main factors taken into reckoning as exingencies as effecting freight and transport and the necessity to curtail the Nation's normal consumption so as to adjust it to the needs of the situation. The urgency of the position allows of no delay in informing the country of what is demanded of it. The public require and desire to have the need explained to them, and only by wholehearted co-operation on the part of all can the object in view be achieved.

The three most important staples of daily consumption are Bread, Meat and Sugar, and forethought for the sustenance of the population requires as to whether compulsion is necessary to ensure an equitable distribution and conservation of available supplies. Compulsory rationing to a fixed quantity per head involves an elaborate machinery which in itself absorbs labour, and for that reason alone ought to be avoided unless absolutely necessary. Therefore, having carefully weighed the advantages and disadvantages, I have come to the conclusion that a voluntary system is preferable until further experience is gained, and meanwhile to rely on the Nation's instinct of self discipline. The allowance indicated is based on the average weekly consumption of each of the commodities which should be permitted to each person. After consideration of the available stocks and probable means of further supplies, the situation requires that the Heads of Families should endeavour to limit themselves to the weekly purchase for each person comprising the household of the following quantities per head:

> Bread 4lbs
> (or its equivalent in flour, 3lbs for bread making)
> Meat .... 2 1/2 lbs
> Sugar .... 3/4 lb

The consumption of these commodities varies according to age, sex, occupation and other conditions. The indicated allowance therefore provides for adjustment or apportioning between members of each household in relation to individual needs. It is recognised that some persons eat more bread and less meat than the quantities indicated above, others eat more meat and less bread. In all these cases a resolute effort on the part of each consumer to reduce consumption by at least 1lb of bread or 3/4lb of meat per week, or both, will automatically bring about a saving of over 1,000,000 tons per annum of these foods. As regards bread, especially, the variation in individual consumption is most marked. That is attriibutable to the fact that the lower the scale of income and the consequent living, the higher the bread consumption, for many in these circumstances meat is only intermittently comprised in the scale of dietary, whereas bread constitutes the main staple. Although these quantities will form the basis of the dietary scale, they will naturally be supplemented by other food products. The Nation is placed upon its honour to observe these conditions. The effect upon consumption will reveal itself through the statistical returns available to the Food Controller. Meanwhile, to meet the contingency that rationing may become necessary the machinery to bring such a system into operation is being organised, so that if and when required we may be ready. It is expected that a patriotic endeavour will be made by everyone to limit consumption wherever possible to below the standard indicated, and by so doing render rationing unnecessary.

   The Food Controller is confident that every individual will cooperate loyally. To the women of the country, who, in this emergency can excercise so much influence, a special appeal is made. Economy is not only a patriotic duty but a necessity. Extravagance is obviously unpatriotic. The power to purchase does not constitute the right, and nobody should obtain more than is necessary to suffice.

   Frugality practised at home will ensure a sufficient supply to all, despite any effort of the enemy, and, as hitherto, a needed provision for our soldiers and sailors. There is hardly a household that has not a direct interest in some loved one fighting for the Nation's honour. Nor is comparison made between their

their sacrifice and suffering and the demand which these conditions will impose on those who enjoy at home the security their valour has established. Every act of self-denial here is a help and aid to those fighting for us on land and sea.

LORD DEVONPORT
Food Controller
Ministry of Food

Understanding the ways of our forebears is essential. At the end of the 20th century we are bombarded on all sides about the rights and wrongs of our food intake. In 1917 such sophistication was unknown and with the above plea from the Food Controller came an "explanatory note". It explained that; *"meat includes bacon, ham, sausages, game, rabbits, poultry and tinned meat. The ration of 2 1/2 lbs per head per week means uncooked meat as bought from the butcher and includes bone and fat. Housekeepers are expected to reduce their household consumption in respect of members of their household who take their meals away from home. The allowance of flour for bread making is expected to include that used for cakes, puddings etc. It is recognised that some housewives will not be able to afford to buy the full allowance of meat and may consequently be compelled to exceed the bread allowance of 4lbs per head per week. In such cases they are expected to keep their purchases of bread at least 1lb per head below their previous consumption."*

> Readers might be interested in the week's average rations for one person in World War Two. 2 pints of milk, 4 ozs bacon, just under 1lb of meat, 1/4 lb butter, 2 ozs cheese, 1/2 lb sugar, 2 ozs lard, 4 ozs margarine, 1/2 lb jam, 2ozs tea, 1 egg, 3ozs sweets.

Cuckfield's V.A.D Hospital (Queen's Hall) was extremely busy. The ladies of Cuckfield regularly organised charity events to raise money to help its needs. In their March meeting the Urban District Council considered a request from Dr Wells to increase the capacity of the hospital. By using the recreation room, and using the reading room for recreation, ten more patients could be accommodated.

The following letter appeared in the *Mid Sussex Times:* . . .

Sir, - The Cuckfield V.A.D Hospital makes its first appeal for help to the public. Please help us! The patients get well so quickly at Cuckfield (373 were received in 1916) that orders have come from Headquarters that ten more beds must be provided. Structural alterations and additional equipment make it expensive, and we want £250 – and as much more as we can get! Every little helps, and big sums help even more; but if all do all they can then the result will be a success. Staplefield and Haywards Heath - will help their old mother! - (Cuckfield) Subscriptions may be sent either to me or straight to the Capital Bank, Haywards Heath.

Signed, on behalf of the Committee, M A Cooper. Tentercroft, Cuckfield.

Relatives "back home" must have longed to hear from their loved ones serving overseas, sometimes hundreds of miles away. Typically the recipient would have the letter reproduced in the local paper so that friends and neighbours could share the news. For the vast majority of the townspeople of Cuckfield, like so many in 1917, travel abroad was unthinkable. Letters like the one below from Corporal E Mitchell, R E, to his father W E Mitchell would have been very interesting and informative about the war far away; Published in the *Mid Sussex Times* was, A LETTER FROM MESOPOTAMIA, written on Jan 11th:

> There are no roads here, and when it rains things are awful. There is a difficulty in getting the food up, but we never go short. It is very good food, and we get bread and fresh meat. The weather is very cold and wet now, just as bad as it was in France, though they say that it is better than the heat in summer. But still, that is not for three months yet, and a lot may happen before then. The Tigris has risen a bit lately, but I do not think the country will be flooded, as we have erected embankments, or, as they call them "bunds", by the river side. The country is horribly monotonous, as it is dead level and not a shrub or blade of grass in sight. We can see a range of mountains about 50 miles away to the East. At present their tops are covered with snow, and they look fine when the sun shines on them in the early morning. I have heard a lot about General Townshend's defence of Kut and of the attempts to relieve him. I hope to be able to tell you something about it some day. There are plenty of jackals and hyenas about. They come round sometimes in the camps at night looking for grub. The Turks do not seem to have artillery, and when the few they have start they are usually shut up quickly by ours. We have plenty. We also have monitors on the river, and they occasionally let rip with their big guns. The Turks are jolly good scrappers and very clean fighters. They have a few aeroplanes, but they do not do much. We do pretty well what we like in the air. We are very short of smokes just now, and I should be glad if you would pack up a few in a parcel.

> Kut was a small town in Mesopotamia (Iraq). The Turks abandoned it in October 1915. General Townshend's 6th Indian Division made a stand there after retreating from the north in November. It was difficult to defend as the attacking army had the advantage of good field positions in the surrounding flood plains. In addition, the Anglo-Indian forces were exhausted. With reasonable food supplies General Townshend thought he could hold out for two months and the C-in-C Mesopotamia, General Nixon was confident in relieving the town in that time. The Turks initially lost a large number of troops to the British machine guns. In consequence, they concentrated their efforts to blocking the relief attempts, maintaining a blockade of Kut with a small holding force. The battle raged beyond the two months, incurring many casualties on both sides. There were light bombing raids by German planes. British planes dropped supplies in April 1916 and there was an attempt to bring supplies up river by a boat, which was the last realistic chance for the defenders. General Townshend surrendered on April 30th 1916. On February 24th 1917, a new army under General Maude, recaptured Kut.

To help with the war effort and to encourage women to seek employment a Creche was available. Its committee published a report thanking all those who contributed to the expenses of the nursery through the house to house collection that had raised £6. They said that sixty to seventy children regularly attended each week and that the scheme was considered a great success. Further, most of the toys were now worn out and there was an appeal for replacements.

The Creche started in April 1916 at Richmond Villa, Whiteman's Green. The notice advertising the service, called upon mothers who wanted to go out to work in these difficult times, to leave their children in capable hands. The charges were 4d one child, 6d two children and 8d for three. These prices included breakfast, dinner and tea, and supervision from 8am until 6pm.

In Cuckfield Park there was a War Hospital Supply Depot administered by Mrs Preston and staffed by women from Cuckfield. The work was to provide items for hospitals. Since it started it had produced, 2136 roller bandages, 776 sewn bandages, 158 pairs of pyjamas, 339 sunshields, 3142 swabs and a variety of other things in demand at hospitals. Mrs Preston was always looking for more regular helpers.

A letter recently received from the regional headquarters of the War Hospital Supply Depots in Brighton, to which Cuckfield was affiliated asked for more help. The Superintendent, Mrs Bromley-Davenport wrote:

> Dear Mrs Preston, I do not know if at present your district has been canvassed for educated women to fill shells. Here this week at HQ we have been asked for 30,000 for this work. Women between 18 and 30 who are only putting in half time at the depot and doing no other war work and are strong enough to help the

country in its hour of need by filling shells. We very much want you to appeal to workers in your district to sacrifice and give up all that is not the sternest duty, to do their duty at the depot. Those who remain must do double work to fill the place of those who have gone. During the next three months our depots will have demands made upon them that one is almost afraid to contemplate . . .

> Probably the greatest need for women was to work in munitions factories. In 1915 there was an acute shortage of shells. Government intervention resulted in the conversion of hundreds of factories to manufacture them. By 1918 several hundred thousand women had been recruited for factory work. Conditions were not only arduous but extremely dangerous. The workers were nick-named "canary girls", because the TNT used for filling shells turned hands and faces yellow. Small explosions were everyday occurances but there were also some major disasters. Huge explosions at Chilwell and Silvertown killed hundreds.

On March 27th news came, that Sergeant M Anscombe, (Pat Anscombe's father) wounded last July had received his discharge from the army. This was after being in hospital for nine months with a fractured foot. The *Mid Sussex Times:* - "Mike" has undergone not a few trying experiences at the Front, but it must ever remain to him a happy recollection that when his Country called for men he promptly answered: he did his bit!

In July 1916 Sgt Anscombe had written a letter home published in the paper. In it he recounts that fateful day when he was wounded.

> Just a few lines to let you know I have been wounded in the left leg and right foot. I am glad to say the wounds are not serious. I am in the base hospital at present, but expect to go to "Blighty" in a day or so. Our division got called up again after a few days' rest, and on the night of the 14th we went up to a wood where a lot of fighting had been going on. Our lot drove the Germans out of it. We were supposed to dig a trench and wire it to stop the enemy's counter attack, but we got shelled so heavily that it was next to an impossible job, so we took what cover we could in shell holes and waited. It was there that I got hit. There were five of my section in this shell hole when another shell dropped straight in. We all got wounded, but not seriously. Frank Elphick and Harry Chatfield who used to work at Denman's were two out of the five. I haven't heard yet how the other Cuckfield boys got on, they are in different companies.

Mike Anscombe underwent an operation on July 16th. His "not too serious" wounds suffered during the Somme offensive, resulted in his discharge a year later.

At a meeting of the Cuckfield Rural Council's Tribunal, the military were seeking the review of a number of men, with certificates of exemption. It was urged that the respondents would be doing a greater service for their country in the army than by remaining in civilian employment. This was a lengthy meeting and the army was successful in some cases. In 1917 details of the working of the tribunals featured very highly in the everyday life of the townspeople. The members were only human, and they were being asked to pass judgement upon their neighbours. They were under great pressure to send more and more men to fill the ranks of soldiers the Generals required. Two unsuccessful appeals are worth pondering. The first, represented by a solicitor, Mr Donne, was the case of an auctioneer and land agent from Haywards Heath. He had been passed for C3 service (the lowest grade), and it was claimed that his occupation was in the national interest. The military application was refused, and exemption granted. The second case concerned a grocer's wharehouseman in Ardingly. Again, represented by Mr Donne, the applicant had passed for C3 service. Knowing the man's physical defects, Mr Donne suggested that it was remarkable that he had been passed for any form of service. He had a clubbed foot, a withered arm and paralysed down the left side. The applicant was asked to walk across the room and it was at once decided to grant him total exemption, subject to the provision of his medical certificate.

It is small wonder that those combatants able to commit their thoughts to paper should feel the need to express themselves, particularly following their own experiences in the trenches.

MEMORIAL TABLET - Siegfried Sassoon M.C.
(Great War)

Squire nagged and bullied till I went to fight,
(Under Lord Derby's Scheme). I died in hell –
(They called it Passchendaele). My wound was slight,
And I was hobbling back; and then a shell
Burst slick upon the duck-boards: so I fell
Into the bottomless mud, and lost the light.

At sermon-time, while Squire is in his pew,
He gives my gilded name a thoughtful stare;
For, though low down upon the list, I'm there;
"In proud and glorious memory"... that's my due.
Two bleeding years I fought in France, for Squire:
I suffered anguish that he's never guessed.
Once I came home on leave: and then went west ...
What greater glory could a man desire?

The War Goes On

Continuing the war in summary, we can draw upon well-documented information to tell us what really happened. The people at home then were trying to come to terms with their increasing difficulties, and the scant news of their loved ones.

"THAT WAS A BIT O' SHRAPNEL BILL."
"SHRAPNEL BE BLOWED! NOW I KNOW WHERE THAT XMAS PUDDEN FROM 'OME WENT TO!"
(WITH APOLOGIES.)

I sit and gaze in the firelight gleam—
You are my longing and you my dream!

Above a typical postcard from home.

The year 1917 was the nadir of the war for both sides. It was 'going nowhere' and war weariness was paramount. All talk of peace had collapsed. The first quarter of the year saw a period of relative calm on the Western Front. There were constant skirmishes in the small towns and villages and the dreadful trench warfare was always there.

On January 31st Germany announced that it was to restart its unrestricted submarine warfare campaign. The German High Command had reasoned that Britain would submit to starvation before effective American participation. To date the USA had been reluctant to come into the war, but on February 3rd it broke off diplomatic relations with Germany.

Overall command of the Allied forces in France and Belgium went to the French General, Robert Nivelle. During the defence of Verdun in 1916, he established his reputation and position. He claimed by massively extending his innovative 'creeping-artillery barrages' tactics the war would be effectively won in 48 hours of a new offensive. Thus the Nivelle Offensive was planned for the spring of 1917, the French attacking the Germans in Artrois and Champagne and the British attacking at Arras.

On February 21st until the end of March the Germans carried out Operation Alberich. This comprised the tactical withdrawal of their forces, from the Arras-Soisson sector, to the Hindenberg Line defensive system. This prevented an early attack planned by the Allies.

British forces recaptured the Mesopotamian town of Kut on February 24th. It had fallen to the Turks in April 1916 after a lengthy siege. The victory at Kut preceded the march on Baghdad, the Ottoman Empire's southern capital. It fell to Anglo-Indian troops on March 17th (Cpl Mitchell's letter, page 38).

Tsar Nicholas II of Russia abdicated on March 15th following the February revolution. Russia's prolonged involvement in the war was doomed. The Tsar was arrested, and finally executed after the October Revolution.

The important French warship, the *Danton*, was sunk after being torpedoed by a U Boat off Corfu in March.

On the Palestine Front the first battle of Gaza took place in March. It was a confused action, both sides really unable to understand the other's true strength or position. The result seemed to suggest to the Turkish commander General Kressanstein that the battle was lost. He was wrong, but this prevented him from calling up reserves that would probably give him a victory. British losses were about 4,000 against 2,400 Turkish and German casualties. Information reaching London told of greater enemy losses thus presenting a victory, prompting support for a renewed offensive.

Although the fighting in other theatres of war was being prosecuted, the war was only going to be decided on the Western Front. Local battles were taking place virtually daily, but the build up to the spring offensive was the main objective.

Difficult to comprehend is the fact that so many men were killed, in securing or perhaps more accurately, fighting over such small parcels of land. Such was the superiority of the defensive positions that to win the war, which meant being the attacker, the numbers of fighting men required just grew and grew.

> Not one corner of a foreign field
> But a span as wide as Europe;
> An appearance of a titan's grave,
> And the length thereof a thousand miles,
> It crossed all Europe like a mystic road,
> Or as the Spirits' Pathway lieth on the night.
> And I heard a voice crying
> This is the Path of Glory.
> **Wilfred Owen. M.C.**

3
APRIL - JUNE 1917
More Home Events

April began and the plea for the new National Service movement continued a pace. The country's civilian population was being exhorted on all sides to 'do its bit'. The Director General of the National Service placed a letter in the press setting out the objects of the operation. He told how every "Patriotic Citizen from 18 to 61" could help in the war effort. He said that:

> The object of the general appeal for volunteers is to form a register of willing workers. The request is for men to sign a voluntary offer of service, so that they may be asked to undertake work of national importance if they are wanted and when they are wanted. The signing of the enrolment form poses on the volunteer a moral obligation to keep his promise. It does not involve him in any legal consequence. It is the intention of the Department that volunteers shall be so placed that they shall have the minimum of inconvenience and the maximum of pay for the work which they are asked to undertake. The minimum wage of 25s a week was fixed so that men should not be asked to work at the low rate of wages prevailing in some agricultural districts. The Prime Minister announced that the minimum wage for agricultural labour is to be raised to 25s in all districts by legislation. A volunteer was entitled to claim 17s.6d subsistence allowance if asked to move away from home. All skilled tradesman who are entitled to enrol as munitions workers are advised to do so, as they gain certain advantages thereby. (There was no mention of what those advantages were). The Government have introduced this system of voluntary National Service in the hope of avoiding any necessity for a compulsory scheme.

Pressure on the people at home increased with an appeal directed at the women who volunteered for National Service. They were promised recognition of their efforts. A woman's role in society had always been clearly defined, but war was hastening the day of change. Women who volunteered under the scheme were, after selection enrolled in the Women's Land Army, each member becoming a war land worker. A worker could expect promotion to group-leader if proficient, and, receive higher wages and be given a distinctive arm band inscribed with the word "leader". A group leader may become an instructor in a training centre, receive yet more pay and wear a distinctive armlet bearing the title of "instructor". A further inducement was the prospect of selected members wishing to continue a career on the land, after the war, would be registered separately. Then every effort would be the Dominions abroad. The National Service Department declared its support and encouragement to women to make *"the best of themselves"*. How many were to avail themselves of this offer?

The Reverend Maddock was now back in Cuckfield following his voluntary service with the YMCA. At his evening service on Sunday 8th April he gave an account of his work in "Message from the Front". He actually preached that evening in his YMCA uniform and the hymns chosen were the soldiers' favourites from his services in Flanders. He took for his text 1. Samuel xvii, 17-18, the story of Jesse sending his son David to go down to thy camp to "look how thy brethren fare, and take their pledge." He likened that to his own situation, saying *"I went as your representative to assure the men that the Churches in England were solicitous for their welfare, and would grudge no sacrifice to serve and comfort them."* The congregation in the packed church was told that for three months he had been within range of German guns. He had seen the men in their huts, on parade and marching to the trenches and back again. *"I took a message from the Church and it was worth the Church's while to send their ministers, if only to serve cocoa, cakes and tobacco in a white collar".* Reverend Maddock hoped that the soldiers' homecoming, would be all they wished. When he arrived home the previous Friday, said *"It was the fairest place I have ever seen in dream or reality."*

This type of message was what the folk back home wanted to hear. First hand experiences of people like the Reverend Maddock, whether they related to men from Cuckfield or not, would have meant so much to them. There were certainly no radio and television reporters beaming back accounts of the action as it happened. News was hard to come by, letters were heavily censored. Conditions at home, with food shortages forever the subject of press propaganda, deteriorated. The result was a plethora of meetings compelling everybody to do more.

On April 6th America declared war on Germany, which must have been received with delight. The *Mid Sussex Times* reported the matter on April 10th with the headline as shown.

It was not until the spring of 1918 that the American Expeditionary Force arrived in Europe. The immediate impact of the announcement of the 6th was to step up the supply of materials to the allies. The US unleashed its vast industrial potential. It is estimated that Britain alone received almost one billion bullets, 31 million shells and 1.2 million rifles. It should be remembered of course that all this had to be paid for.

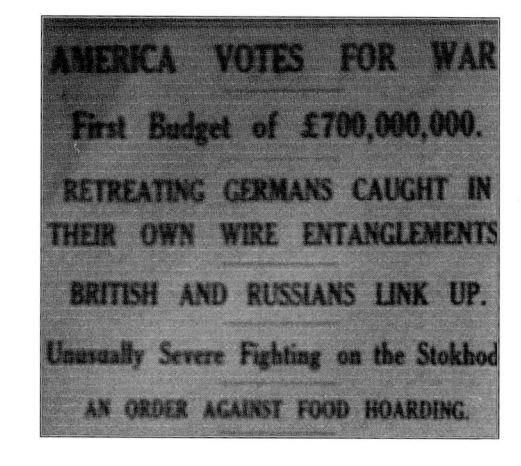

AMERICA VOTES FOR WAR
First Budget of £700,000,000.
RETREATING GERMANS CAUGHT IN THEIR OWN WIRE ENTANGLEMENTS
BRITISH AND RUSSIANS LINK UP.
Unusually Severe Fighting on the Stokhod
AN ORDER AGAINST FOOD HOARDING.

Letters home were always well received. Many recipients, as we have seen, happily shared the contents with others, often by having them published in the *Mid Sussex Times*. Another such letter from Sapper H Martin to his mother Mrs Martin of Burgess Hill was so typical, extracts follow:

> It has been 'some' push here! I recollect in one of our last moves five of us had to go forward on bicycles, and it was nothing but scrape, scrape the mud off every ten yards. You should have seen the mess we were in. Taking bicycles over trenches, barbed wire etc, it was a game, I can assure you, and we got simply plastered with mud, even to the underclothing . . . I went over' no man's land' the other day and picked a large bunch of snowdrops. I didn't get potted at. One day the Huns were within a quarter of a mile of us, and two days later they had hopped off 15 miles, so, of course we had to follow them. They left plenty of helmets behind them, but we did not pick them up, as nearly all of them had bombs underneath which exploded when the helmet was lifted. We have had quite an experience the last few days
> . . . We are now back in 'rest' at a town about the same size as Three Bridges. Our soldiers are very brave . . . There is a cheeriness that makes you glad in the worst of places. The best of all is knowing that you have a great and good Protector watching over you, and knowing that you are committed to His care makes you have such a feeling of happiness and security that no one else can imagine.

This letter will have given comfort to some at home.

The Cuckfield Urban District Council's April meeting yielded a variety of matters. It was noted and approved, that J Denman & Co. of Broad Street motor car builders, Charles Gibbs & Co. motor car repairers of Whteman's Green and B Burtenshaw of South Street, be allowed the renewal of their petrol licences.

The Council had instructed the clerk, Mr C H Waugh, to apply to the Ministry of Munitions for leave to purchase tar from Cuckfield Gas Works for use upon the roads.

A plan was approved for additional sanitary accommodation in the VAD Hospital, an extra bath and bed-pan washing equipment.

The surveyor, Mr Albert Croucher, reported that he made the weekly pig food collection. Unfortunately it never exceeded four buckets weekly, but that as the season advanced perhaps the supply would increase. This was a collection of scraps for use at the Council's pig farm.

There was a plea for less noise! A number of residents (not named) had lately complained of the hideous noise made by the cadet buglers, and the matter brought to the attention of the C.O. In the old days, it was said, the buglers went into the fields far away from dwellings to practice. There was no reason they should not do so again.

Mr Stephen Knight confirmed that at the next meeting he would be moving that the Council make a grant of £25 to the 7th Battalion Sussex Volunteer Regiment.

Members of the Council present were Mr R Anscombe JP Chairman, Miss Payne, Messrs S Knight, C Hobson, T I Symons, H Bates, J Denman, E Napper, B Burtenshaw, the clerk, Mr C H Waugh and the surveyor Mr A Croucher.

A Voluntary Work Organisation, the VWO, had been formed. Its purpose was to carry out tasks, such as, the work at the War Hospital Supply Depot at Cuckfield Park. It was a womens' organisation. Mrs S R Clarke the President, Mrs Vaughan the Treasurer, Mrs Wilson the Secretary and Miss F Mitchell, Miss Cleare, Miss E Payne, Mrs A Burtenshaw, Mrs Huckett, Mrs Maddock, Mrs Wilson and Miss Payne were on the Depot committee.

The importance of the church in the community cannot be over emphasised and the significance of Easter was demonstrably shown by the commitment of all churchgoers.

On Good Friday the Wesleyan Church held its anniversary service, conducted by a special preacher Pastor G Millar of St John's, Burgess Hill. A tea followed the anniversary meeting in the evening. Mr G E Thompson presided and Mr Charles Pearse of Pilstye Farm, the treasurer, presented an encouraging report. The Reverend Maddock and J Murray spoke interestingly to the gathering.

At the Congregational Church on Good Friday evening the choir performed *"The Crucifixion"*. Soloists were, Mrs L Bennett and Mr G Miles, Mr Fred Knight the music teacher played the organ.

The Parish Church on Good Friday morning held the Three Hours' service and in the evening, the choir sang the cantata *"Olivet to Calvary"*. Soloists were Mr H Inman (tenor) and Mr G H Fowler (baritone), the organist Mr T E P Attewell. The first evensong of Easter was on Saturday.

On Easter Sunday the spire of Cuckfield Church had a narrow escape from being destroyed by fire. Shortly after the service had begun Mr A Browne, the clerk, went up into the battlements to haul down the flag. Upon opening the door onto the battlements, he was met by a spurt of flame, finding that the woodwork by the door was alight. He summoned help from Mr W E Mitchell, the churchwarden, Mr W Robinson, his brother Bert and one or two others. They extinguished the fire. The lead had to be torn away from the doorway, but not before some of it had become fused. Fortunately the general damage was slight due to the prompt action of Mr Browne. There was no doubt that the spire and the Church had been in grave danger. During this excitement the service had continued without the congregation knowing about the fire!.

A few days later an enquiry declared that the church exits needed improving. The doors opened inwards and were too narrow. It was left with the Vicar and the Churchwardens to consider the matter. No verdict was given on the likely cause of the fire.

At a meeting, the Guardians of West Hylands the Poor Law Institution, said they were asked to provide emergency beds for the military. These were needed for the expected increase in the number of wounded soldiers.

The Cuckfield Parish Church Bellringer's Association held its annual meeting. The Hon. Secretary Mr F Hounsell, Senior, reported that ten of its members were on military service, Messrs F and E Attwater (married in March, page 33), G Apps, A Chinnery, F Mitchell, F E Mitchell, T Mitchell, R Gibson, F Hounsell jnr, A Wheale and G Woods. This sadly left only five members of the association left to ring. Condolences were expressed to Mr and Mrs Gibson on the death of their son. The formation of a Ladies section was approved.

On April 15th there was a special Thanksgiving service. Canon Wilson gave thanks for the preservation of the spire, and the church, from destruction on Easter Sunday. Further evidence of the importance of the pulpit, in the context of war information, came, when the worshippers were given a progress report on the state of the war. The vicar spoke out about the victories in Palestine, Egypt and the Western Front.

In the *Mid Sussex Times* of April 24th a letter appeared under the heading, *"Photographs, can you oblige?"* The gist of which stated – Many people must have photographs of those parts of Belgium and France now occupied by the enemy. Photographs and picture postcards of places including bridges, railway junctions, rivers, canals and factories etc, would be of great use to the government. Owners who are willing to donate them should forward them to the relevant authority.

The celebrations at the school for Empire Day were marked by two major events, the re-erection of the flagpole and a unique proclamation by the children. The first flagpole was given to the school in 1906 by Mr James Rowland a local builder. This followed a plea that the school *"would not be happy until some kind friend had given a flagstaff and flags, so that the boys could be taught patriotism"*. Mr Herrington the headmaster had seen it taught in Canada and the United States. Unfortunately the pole was blown down in the autumn gales of 1916, but Mr Rowlands came to the rescue in time for Empire Day. Two hundred children stood in their playground beneath the flag and another two hundred visitors, parents and children lined the path in the churchyard. Forty little seven-year olds standing in a semi circle were each carrying a flag representing the Empire and all the nations of Europe, except the enemy. In addition and prominently displayed was the Stars and Stripes. Then came the ceremony, inspired by Private F Anscombe, on leave, introduced by Mr Herrington as an old boy. On his command the flag was saluted and all the children raised their separate flags making the proclamation of allegiance. *"Flag of our Country and of the Empire, Inspirer in battle, Protector of our Homes, whose crosses remind us of St George, St Andrew and St Patrick, we Salute Thee. We born under thy folds, do pledge our hearts, lives and our sacred honour, to love and protect Thee, Flag of our Country and Empire forever."* The uniqueness of this event as claimed by the school was that, as far as was known, no other children in the British Isles were doing the same. It was claimed, that in its three hundred years' history, the school had probably never seen or heard any celebration to compare with Empire Day of 1917.

The Annual General Meeting of the Cuckfield Urban District Council was held on May 3rd and Mr R Anscombe was unanimously re-elected Chairman for the ensuing year. The other councillors were, Miss E Payne and Messrs S Knight, H Bates, B J Burtenshaw, S Caffyn, E E Napper, T I Symans, A Beeching, C Hobson and J Denman, Mr C H Waugh the clerk and Mr A Croucher the surveyor. In Mr Anscombe's acceptance speech he hoped that the coming year would bring the joy of lasting peace. The committees were elected, including the Emergency Committee. (Their duties not specified). The Farm Committee's special task was to administer allotments, the surveyor reporting, there were no vacant plots at present. Mr Burtenshaw remarked that some were of 40 or 50 roods (one rood equals a quarter of an acre). There were many applications for plots. The Clerk was instructed to purchase a potato spraying machine from the Board of Agriculture. The Surveyor reported that according to instructions he had dug up the ground, as far as requested, by the wives of servicemen. Mr Clapp of Courthouse Farm had successfully tendered for horse hire. The surveyor was instructed to arrange with Mr Clapp for the Council's horse to be employed where possible. The surveyor was further instructed to obtain such horse hire as he could for the roads at 1s 6d per hour for one horse and man. The Emergency Committee was to be consulted upon failure to find work. Mr Preece of Lower Sparks Farm, had made an acceptable offer of £9, for the middle bed of grass on the Sewage Farm.

On May 2nd, what today would be a controversial matter, the Sparrow Club held its AGM at the King's Head. Not an appreciation society, it was concerned with the "very good work" of keeping the sparrow population under control. Lighthearted by comparison with the dreadful war taking place the aims of the club would today find many a critic. It is worth recounting some detail. Subscribers to the club were landowners and others who wanted to keep down the number of sparrows. The yearly tariff was 5s over 100 acres, 2s 6d for less than 100 acres and 1s for an ordinary garden. Payment to club members was made for the number of birds' heads and eggs presented to designated officials. The total number of old birds' heads brought in was 2,799, young birds' heads 666 and eggs 1,288. The champion for 1916 was Mr A Beeching with the grand score of 935, 169 and 444 respectively, for which he received £2. 3s.4d. Members spoke of the damage done by house sparrows and other birds and that the Government was urging the destruction of certain birds.

It seems however, that the members of the Sparrow Club found their activity a sport as well as so-called pest control.

A letter from the Royal Society for the Protection of Birds was published in the *Mid Sussex Times*

> Sir, - As it has been pointed out by the Board of Agriculture that the destruction of insect eating birds at the present time would gravely endanger our food crops, may I invite your readers to send for copies of "Birds, Insects and Crops", which

gives practical information as to work done by certain birds. The statement by the Board that house sparrows only, are the proper object of sparrow clubs etc, indicates theabsolute necessity for prohibiting children from killing birds and taking eggs, since they ransack the hedgerows where house sparrows do not build, and destroy the insect eating birds, every one of which is the ally of the food producer, and will be badly needed by him this summer. May I also beg householders to spare the nests of house martins and swallows, whose work as sanitary agents is invaluable to the community. A little sand or gravel below the nest, if this is in the porch or over the doorsteps, will obviate any trouble during the short time the young are in the nest.

Yet again in the news were the worries about food shortages. The one issue dominating all others was bread consumption. The Corn Production Bill had its second reading in the House of Commons, the Government finally taking a direct part in production, rather than leaving the matter in the hands of the free market. Consumers were asked by the Food Controller to cut consumption of bread by a quarter. Non combatants could show their patriotism, *"Much as he loved the staff of life, he loved his country more." – Punch Magazine.*

The matter had become a crisis and one course of action was to hold a public meeting and bring people together to share the problem. At one such meeting in Burgess Hill, entitled "Economise in Food and Win the War" many speakers made fervent appeals for restraint. None more so than Mr Bayliss, whose words under the heading of "Victory", declared:

Compulsory rationing would not be fair, the expense would be enormous. The remedy for the difficulty was voluntary food rationing. The military problem had been solved, we could beat the Germans on the land. The naval problem had been solved, we could beat the Germans on the sea. The financial problem had been solved, our money would outlast the German's money. The food problem remained, it was for the women with the help of the men to solve it. The housekeeper's cupboard was the trench and the housewives must defend it. She must pit her knowledge against the Germans as effectively as the British soldier pointed his gun. If we had an army well fed and a navy well fed we would secure victory which would bring us lasting peace and England's sons will not have died in vain. A little simplistic perhaps, but as a rallying call it drew much applause.

In Cuckfield there were two meetings on the subject. The first, held in the Congregational Schoolroom, was under the auspices of the Cuckfield Women's Suffrage Society and the Wivelsfield Women's Institute. Mrs Godman, the President of the Wivelsfield Institute, herself a keen suffragist, addressed the packed hall and gave an account of the workings of their group. The Wivelsfield Institute was founded a year ago with 25 members and now boasted one hundred. She explained some of their activities. They met each month, discussed matters of interest in the home, and were presently involved in the question of food production and economy. There was an active exchange of recipes and hints on the renovation of clothes etc. They had a War Savings Association. They went in for herb collection and had sent large quantities to a manufacturing chemist in London. The Institute drew the women together in these "hard times", they were doing their bit and gave them something interesting to write about to the men at the front.

Miss Elizabeth Robins from Louisville, Kentucky, an actress and author gave a talk. She was on a lecture tour of England, by invitation of the Ministry of Food. Her topic was "War Economy and Food Rations". She gave an impassioned performance regarding the seriousness of the food shortage and how necessary it was to avoid waste. She told her audience that the wheat crop in wheat producing countries had failed resulting in a world wide shortage. The submarine menace had made the situation worse. The Germans regarded the British as a wasteful nation, and it was now recognised, that before the war the country could be fed on what it wasted. There was a great need to economise on wheat flour and more use should be made of pulses, young dandelion leaves, young dock leaves and nettle tops. Miss Robins made the same plea as others that compulsory rationing was undesirable. Women could solve the problem and women at the cooking range could do as important a service as the men behind the guns.

The second meeting was a War Cooking Demonstration at the Parish Room, sponsored by Mrs Preston and Dr McConnell. The speaker was Mrs Anderson from the National Food Economy League who also gave a practical cookery demonstration. Some of the rhetoric was really hard, it was said that a person not prepared for self sacrifice, was *"a selfish, cold blooded thing – a Pro German. The men were contemplating another winter at the front and it was the duty of those at home to see that whoever went without, it was not the men who were facing all kinds of perils to keep the Germans from our shores."* Finally Mrs Anderson showed some food she had prepared and on a table there were displayed a day's rations for a working man.

> Breakfast – One egg, 3ozs margarine, 1/2 ozs jam/marmalade, coffee and milk 7ozs.
> Dinner – 5 1/2ozs meat, 2 ozs onion, carrot & turnip, 1oz unpearled barley, 4 ozs greens,
> 1 oz of bread and 5 ozs of milk pudding.
> Tea – 1 oz bread, oatcake (1oz oatmeal), 1/2 oz margarine, 1/2 oz jam, tea and milk 3 oz
> Supper/Lunch – 2 ozs bread, 4 ozs fish, 1/4 oz margarine, 1 oz cheese, 5 ozs stewed fruit.

A comment made suggested that the dinner appeared ample but the breakfast did not look very substantial for a person expected to do a hard day's work. (A comparison with the ration allowances during the Second World War on page 37 makes interesting reading).

At a special meeting the Urban District Council formed a National Service Committee as required by the National Service Department. Messrs Anscombe, Knight, Croucher, Bowell and Miss I Turner were appointed. Mr Croucher, the Council's surveyor, was appointed to carry out the duties under the Local Authorities (Food Control) Order. The clerk, was instructed to obtain potato spraying material.

A second frame containing fifteen more photographs of Cuckfield men killed in action was on display at the Queen's Hall, adding to those already on view. (See page 34).

There was mixed news about some of Cuckfield sons. Second Lieutenant Frank Stevens Royal Flying Corps, the eldest son of Mr and Mrs Stevens of Garnalds, was promoted to Lieutenant as Balloon Commander in the Kite Balloon Section.

Lieutenant R S Worsley previously reported as missing, was a prisoner of war in Germany. His letter home stated:

> My pilot and I were brought down by anti-aircraft guns. We were too far over the German lines, and had to fly rather low in order to see the ground, which was obscured by clouds. The engine was hit, so we could not climb to get away. We were surrounded and searched as soon as we reached the ground, having no time to destroy our machine. After two days they took us to Brussels – from here to Cologne, Bonn, Gottenberg, Frankfurt and on to Karlsruhe. We were very well fed and kindly treated.

Sad news arrived, Lieutenant W H Mitchell was lost at sea. As a member of the Inns of Court OTC he was commissioned in the East Surrey Regiment in September 1915. In May 1916 he volunteered for special service in Egypt, attached to the Kings Royal Rifles. He served in Salonika for ten months then transferred to the Royal Flying Corps as a pilot. Returning home through the Mediterranean his ship was torpedoed and he was lost at sea. He was 19 years of age.

Mrs E Dancy heard that her husband was wounded in action while serving with the Egyptian Expeditionary Force. He was the third son of Mr and Mrs W Dancy of Whiteman's Green, one of five sons. The other three were serving with the army, one in France, one in Salonika and one in England. The fifth boy was killed in 1915 in the Dardenelles.

There was a story in the *Mid Sussex Times* of a chance meeting, between one of their reporters, and Private Cecil Cook, son of Mr and Mrs Cook, South Street, Cuckfield. He was home on leave, after twenty-two months in France, and looking as brown as a berry, he said:

> I was almost beside myself with joy when I reached London. It seemed too good to be true.The life and movement, the surroundings and atmosphere were all so different from what I had grown accustomed to across the water." (When asked about the Sussex boys he replied: Very fit most of them, but their spirits would

be gayer if leave were granted them more frequently, say, once in six months. It would put more heart into the chaps. We have gone six months without seeing a civilian, and that was why the sight of London was such a joy to me."

Questioned as to what impressed him most on arriving in France, Private Cook said, *"The slowness of the trains"*. He declared the story to be quite true. One of the men got off the train going from Le Havre to Amiens and milked a cow in a field. He obtained a quart, ran after the train and caught it. Private Cook, with the Royal Sussex Regiment, spoke of Penfold the Burgess Hill footballer, Charlie Boakes of Haywards Heath and Arthur Harding well known in Cuckfield. All of them with the "Sussex". He spoke of the rations. He said, they were better now, one loaf between three men per day, fresh meat three times a week, but lately no potatoes. Claims made for caution in the consumption of food by civilians was not exaggerated. Cecil Cook went on to say, the French made the English soldiers pay enormous prices for things. It was sometimes difficult to get from them even a drink of water without payment. He finished by saying, that *"The Germans do not appear to be short of men, or of guns or of ammunition, and nobody across the water seems to think that the war will end soon."*

More news came of Cuckfield wounded, by now quite a regular event. Corporal W E Mitchell, was invalided home in hospital in Birmingham with enteric fever. Private T Card late of the Ship Inn was on ten days leave after being wounded at Arras. Private Jack Ansell, also on leave, was wounded in the face by shrapnel. The most dramatic story in this section about Cuckfield boys concerned Private G Osborne, reported safely in King George's Hospital, London by his in-laws, Mr and Mrs Meaning. Wounded in the right arm and left side Private Osborne was captured by the Germans. They treated him kindly, bound his wounds and then left him in a trench before leaving. He lay there for four hours. Becoming very thirsty he crawled round the dead bodies of some German soldiers left behind, hoping to find some water in their water bottles. Unfortunately the bottles were empty. After a short time a thunderstorm answered his prayers, and by using a German helmet to collect the water quenched his thirst. With what strength he could muster Private Osborne slowly walked towards the British lines and was discovered by his comrades. After some hours he was carried to a dressing station. At that point, he was told how fortunate he had been, arriving at the British position without being fired upon. The German snipers were very active. It was not to surprising that Private Osborne's nerves were frayed and it was with great relief that he arrived back in Blighty.

Mrs Preston of Cuckfield Park announced that she had ordered 1,200 bottling jars from the appropriate Government department, to encourage the women of Cuckfield to preserve fruit. As the fruit harvest was looking promising she would be making the bottles available at the cost price of 5d each with directions for bottling.

On May 15th an announcement appeared in the *Mid Sussex Times* that caused a considerable amount of interest. It said, that the first week in July, would be declared as National Baby Week.

With the help of Local Government the National Baby Week Council has circularised nearly 2,000 local authorities on the matter. To meet the expenses of the campaign the National Baby Week Council are endeavouring to raise £25,000, and are appealing for public support. Teachers are to be asked to give special lessons during Baby Week, and to allow children to distribute literature. Clergy are asked to have special sermons on Baby Sunday, July 1st, and special meetings in Sunday Schools. It is understood that a bureau of speakers has been arranged, already Balcombe has arranged to do something noteworthy during Baby Week and Cuckfield and Haywards Heath in due course no doubt will put on their thinking caps. Every baby now born is of immense importance to the Empire and every possible effort should be made to give it all opportunities of growing up physically fit. The child of today is the citizen of tomorrow, and on its citizens depends the greatness of the Empire.

In the same paper, the following pieces were printed in the column called "Other men's minds", and were attributed to General Smuts, South African soldier and statesman.

The British Commonwealth – Ours is a commonwealth of nations, I do not like the word empire, it always appals me. The cost of war – It is computed that about eight million people have been killed in the war. Men who should have been creators of a new world. A man made war – This war is man made, it is the result of human force, human intelligence, human stupidity, human greed and ambition.

In a lighter vein, from *Punch Magazine* came, *"Owing to the restrictions on the output of beer", says a contemporary,"the passing of the village inn is merely a question of time." Even before the war it often took hours and hours."*

Following a short closure, the Picture Theatre in Haywards Heath opened at the end of May. Its star attraction was, *"The Patriot of Canada"*, a war film with most realistic war scenes. *"Several times the boys gave vent to their feelings, rising to their feet clapping heartily".*

As an alternative the Brighton entertainment guide had much to offer. At the Theatre Royal Miss Julia Nielson and Mr Fred Terry were starring in *"Sweet Nell of Old Drury"* and *"The Scarlet Pimpernel"*. At the West Pier, *"The Rotters"* and at the Palace Pier *"The Cinema Star"*. The Hippodrome boasted Harry Tate in a new revue entitled *"Goodbye-EE"* and for those who preferred the cinema, the Palladium was showing, *"Under Two Flags"*.

The patients at the VAD Hospital gave a concert on June 2nd. Among the patients there were some very clever entertainers. The promoters were Sergeants Weston and Edwards and Corporal Lehman. As well as the soldiers singing, two lady soloists took part much to the delight of all. Mrs Bannister the matron (below) declared herself very pleased and together with the staff showed much appreciation.

Cuckfield's plans were revealed for the forthcoming Baby Week at a concert given by Mrs Preston at Cuckfield Park. The concert, performed in the drawing room on June 11th, was to raise funds for the proposed Baby Show and Fete. It would be the Park on July 6th. Nearly one hundred people attended, listening to instrumental and vocal items.

At the Urban District Council meeting on June 8th, it was resolved that the Council's own yard, should store coal for public supply for the coming winter. It was decided to look into the matter of water supply to the London Lane allotments. Of somewhat more interest, was to have water turned on at the drinking fountain, erected to the memory of Captain C W Sergison, also to provide a white enamel mug and chain. Readers may recall, that in 1897, when the great debate was taking place regarding a memorial to commemorate Queen Victoria's Diamond Jubilee, a drinking fountain was one proposal. This suggestion was ridiculed at the meeting called to discuss the various possibilities and it never made the short list. From *"A Century Ago"* –

> A Drinking Fountain had been proposed, but amid laughter Major Maberly said he never found anyone availing themselves of a drink from a village fountain except perhaps tramps, and they were not really welcome in the parish. Captain Sergison who died in 1911, actually chaired that first meeting.

The workings of the Cuckfield Tribunals have featured earlier. As suggested, the role of the undoubted layman, to decide the future of his 'neighbour' may not have been easy. To assist members of the tribunal, the civil servants in Whitehall occasionally issued instructions to the tribunal clerks. By the early summer in 1917 it was clear that the intention was to ensure that as many men as possible were available to fight. A recent memorandum indicated that membership of the Volunteer Force or even the Special

Constabulary was no longer a reason for exemption from military service. No one could claim exclusion on the grounds of public service alone. A clear recommendation was issued regarding men classified as B2, C2, B3 and C3. They should be considered for agricultural work rather than the Volunteer Force. From June 14th the Board of Agriculture declared that no man certified by the County Agricultural Committee to be already engaged full time on a farm or farm work of national importance was to be posted for service with the Colours or to be called up for medical examination or re-examination. Food was now very much a priority.

At their meetings in June the Rural and Urban Tribunals met to consider more cases. A Cuckfield coal merchant and farmer asked for exemption for his son, aged 18, employed as a carter and carman. The East Sussex War Agricultural Committee had inspected the applicant's farm and declared it to be in a very unsatisfactory condition. The youth was allowed exemption provided that he worked only on the farm. It was further felt that by sending him away the badly cultivated farm would only deteriorate even further. However, regular monthly inspections would take place and the situation reassessed in three months.

On June 15th Lindfield decided to form a branch of the Women's Institute following the example of Wivelsfield and Scaynes Hill.

The late Mrs Knott of Knowle Lodge left an estate of gross value of £22,744. To her gardener, Mr James Simmons she bequeathed £100.

Private Askew, son of Mr and Mrs Askew of Church Street, serving with the Buffs, was reported wounded. Each month in the *Parish Magazine*, all members of the Parish Church wounded, were listed. A very large number of Cuckfield men serving with the forces were wounded. Some were patched-up and returned to duty and others invalided out. Although the list of those killed was officially kept a similar list of wounded is missing. Remember that lists were also held of members of the non-denominational churches. Leslie Askew had been a secretary of the Cuckfield Cricket Club before the war.

Another hardship of the war was that of ensuring supply of coal during the winter. The Urban District Council had decided on the 8th, to make its yard available for stockpiling of coal. Thus, people unable to buy large quantities at a time, could meet their needs in the coming winter acquiring small quantities at a time. Known as the Coal Project its purpose was to assist the local traders rather than compete with them.

A well-known family in Cuckfield for very many years was the Hounsell family. They featured in many of the clubs and societies. Fred Hounsell senior, was the stonemason at the churchyard. He had served in the Volunteers and the Territorials, with whom he had qualified for a long service medal, Fred had been a high profile resident of Cuckfield for many years. On June 19th it was announced that another family member, Sergeant Major T H Hounsell, serving in India with the Surma Valley Light Horse, was promoted to the rank of Captain and Adjutant. He had joined the 15th Hussars in 1894 and left for India in 1899. He also holds a long service medal. Other members of the Hounsell family were serving with the armed forces in France.

The list of wounded kept growing. News reached Mrs E Witham that her husband was in the military hospital with a hand wound. Mr and Mrs Stoner heard that two of their sons were wounded. William with the Royal Sussex Regiment was in the base hospital and Harold, with a shrapnel wound in the thigh, was in hospital in Surrey.

Finally in June another Cuckfield lad sent a very newsy letter from Egypt. Private Jack Bone, whose father used to be the chauffeur at Ockenden before moving to Essex, had been involved in a serious accident being run over by a lorry. He suffered a broken left leg and bruising of the left leg and head. Recovering, he wrote to his brother Eddie:

> I am running up against a few of the Sussex boys just now. The chap in the next bed to me is the postman from Hurstpierpoint, Pavey by name. He is pretty lively now. On May 16th I was reading in bed when I heard someone say, "Hello Boney, what are you doing here?" And blow me if it wasn't Fred Beard from Whiteman's Green. Needless to say we had a long chat. He had a bullet through the face, but the wound is now well and he has gone back to his regiment. I got a lot of news from him about the boys up the line. Joe Jupp has been wounded but he is not here. Wilfred Mitchell, Steve Knight, Lieutenant Pierce and his brother and Captain Reid from Mill Hall are all well at present. The doctor has just been round and dressed my leg, and I feel like a sardine in a tin now. He says the bone is healing up nicely. It is very pleasant to be in a nice bed once more with sheets and a spring mattress. I hope to be able to get up shortly. I could do with a stick of rhubarb to keep the flies and other animals away.

> Not much to me is yonder lane
>   Where I go every day;
> But when there's been a shower of rain
>   And hedge-birds whistle gay,
> I know my lad that's out in France
>   With fearsome things to see
> Would give his eyes for just one glance
>   At our white hawthorn tree.

From – **The Hawthorn Tree by Siegfried Sassoon M.C.**

The Spring Offensive

The much vaunted Nivelle Offensive began on April 9th with the BEF opening the campaign attacking the German positions in Artois, east of Arras. There had been a five day artillery bombardment using nearly three thousand guns firing three times the number of shells as in the build up to the fighting on the Somme prior to July 1st 1916.

The Canadian Corps' capture of Vimy Ridge was the only really significant victory during the six weeks of the Battle of Arras. This was a prized gain at a cost of 14,000 casualties. That event apart the end result of the battle became the familiar slogging match experienced all too often in 1916. The German Hindenberg Line defensive system around Bullecourt was too strong. The Australian infantry suffered its worst single day's losses on the Western Front on April 11th.

On April 14th Field Marshall Haig halted the British attacks to await news of the French offensive, the main thrust of the spring campaign, (Nivelle's 48 hours?). This was the second Battle of the Aisne (the first was in 1914), called the Chemin des Dames Offensive. It involved a massed French assault on the German positions along the River Aisne between Soissons and Reims. The detailed plans of the pending action had unfortunately fallen into the hands of German intelligence. In addition, the massing of more than one million French troops together with a ten day preliminary artillery barrage, left no surprises for the enemy defence. They were dug-in and waiting. The Germans held the high ground and inflicted very heavy punishment on the French, 40,000 casualties on the first day, April 16th. The fighting raged until May 9th and ended as a complete disaster for General Nivelle, no appreciable gains made and nearly 190,000 French casualties.

The British army renewed its action at Arras on April 23rd. Finally, on May 17th with no hope of strategic success, the fighting was abandoned. British losses amounted to 150,000 against an estimated 100,000 Germans, a ratio applauded as a better rate of attrition for the attacking side than normal.

It is frightening to realise, that the BEF's attack was aimed at a front just twelve miles wide. Their gains were measured in hundreds of yards and a quarter of a million men from both sides paid the price. For the French it was worse! General Nivelle's 48 hour victory melted away, he was sacked, the French Army mutinied! This resulted in the British Army having to assume the major attacking role for the rest of the war.

On April 6th the United States declared war on Germany and on the 7th Cuba followed suit. It would not be until well into 1918 before the American Army became an effective fighting force with sufficient numbers of fully trained men.

Full control of the British Army returned to Field Marshall Haig and he used this position to concentrate on his favoured plan. This was to open a campaign in Flanders to win back the high ground overlooking Ypres. Then follow up by driving the Germans from Belgium, gaining a clear coastline all the way to Holland. It was ambitious, but regarded as the possible 'beginning of the end'. The campaign itself, was known as the Third Battle of Ypres, the first two had been successful defensive actions. By the time the fighting was over in 1917 a new name would be added that would rival the carnage of The Somme, Passchendaele. But more of this later, the offensive started on July 31st.

Viewed by some as a precursor to the main campaign in Flanders, the Battle of Messines began on June 7th. The Messines Ridge was a small region of high ground held by the Germans since 1914. It was a natural strongpoint to the southeast of Ypres and its capture would represent a great boost to the chances of an overall British success. General Plumer commanding the British forces there, instituted a plan, by which twenty underground mines were dug. This incorporated 8,000 metres of tunnels, ending beneath the German fortifications. Hundreds of specialist miners were used for this work, the nineteen mines that were finished filled with 600 tons of explosives. Before the battle General Plumer said, *"Gentlemen, we may not make history tomorrow, but we shall certainly change the geography"*. On May 21st over 2,500 guns and heavy mortars pounded the German forward positions for many days, culminating in the mines being detonated on June 7th. The resultant explosion was actually heard in London, the blast killed approximately 10,000 of the enemy. By June 21st the entire Messines salient was in British hands, a significant victory and a greatly published boost to morale.

On June 11th, forced by a pro-allied government, King Constantine of Greece abdicated. He was the Kaiser's brother-in-law and a German sympathiser. This left the way clear for Greece to declare war on the Central Powers on June 29th.

On June 13th the first air raids by the German Gotha bomber took place on London. Thirty aircraft took part but caused little damage.

THE GENERAL - Siegfried Sassoon. M.C.

"Good-morning, good-morning!" the General said
When we met him last week on our way to the line.
Now the soldiers he smiled at are most of 'em dead,
And we're cursing his staff for incompetent swine.
"He's a cheery old card," grunted Harry to Jack
As they slogged up to Arras with rifle and pack.

But he did for them both by his plan of attack.

4
MEMORIES

SCHOOLGIRLS REMINISCE

What could be better when preparing a social history of a period than to include some personal recollections of the time? Eighty-two years on, and school children then, remember a little of their life during the war.

Daisy Keep (Mrs Daisy Rhodes) born in 1909 started school just after the outbreak of the war. A most vivid recollection was waving goodbye to her father at the dock-side before he sailed to France early in 1916. Albert Keep was killed during the ill-fated Somme campaign in July of that year. His last letter to Daisy is shown, with his photograph taken in the back-garden of 'Garlicks'.

Daisy with her mother and sister lived at the shop of her grandparents, Garlicks, at Whiteman's Green. It was a general store with the Wesleyan Chapel on one side and a private residence the other. This photograph was taken a few years later. Witness the Bull-nosed Morris outside the shop.

60   A SMALL TOWN AT WAR

Winifred Lawson (Mrs Winifred Woolven) born in 1908 started school in 1913. She lived in Naldred Cottage on the Borde Hill estate. Her father worked as a carter on the farm. Winifred recalls the soldiers on guard at the railway viaduct and the local women working on the land with their red and green armlets, the Women's Land Army.

To get to school, Winifred and her friends walked through the estate, coming out of the Hanlye Lane entrance. They referred to Hanlye Lane/Ardingly Road as the 'top road'. Passing by the workhouse she recounts the story of how the inmates would greet the children through the railings. Feeling sorry for them, Winifred and her friends would sometimes give them the sandwich lunch prepared for them by their mothers for school. All was not lost however, as there was a big saucepan of soup cooking at the mission room. For a penny they overcame the loss of their midday meal. Frequently on the way to school she would stop and talk to the wounded soldiers at the VAD Hospital.

Living and working on the Borde Hill estate entitled the family to one free pint of milk a day from the estate farm dairy. One of Winifred's jobs was to collect this milk each day on the way home from school. She carried the milk in a can with a handle. One game was to see whether you could swing the can through a circle without any spillage. The occasional calamity is easy to visualise; it happened!

Apparently some of the children who lived in Ansty attending the school were very apprehensive about walking past Cuckfield Park as they believed it haunted. Children being children meant that the braver 'Cuckfield Kids' would follow their Ansty peers as far as the park chanting suitable taunts. Little did they know, the following letter appeared in the *Mid Sussex Times* on January 5th 1917 under the heading, Legend of an Apparition:

> Dear Sir,- I am very interested in reading your account of Mrs Sergison. I should like to know if there is any truth in the legend that after Mrs Sergison was buried her ghost was supposed to have haunted the neighbourhood of Cuckfield, and that a Mr Osborne a Sussex yeoman, of Newtimber Place, and a bit of a sport, would not believe the story until one night he was riding home when his horse stopped suddenly and shivered, and his rider thought he saw an apparition, and dismounting, led the animal some distance before remounting and continuing his journey. After this happened it is stated that a special meeting of the villagers was held at midnight, when the burial service was read backwards to lay the ghost.
> Yours Faithfully, F Carter.
> p.s – Aside – My wife is a great granddaughter of Mr Osborne, through whom I relate this story.

One story believed by children of the time, told how King Charles I hid in a tree in Cuckfield Park. Another, that Dick Turpin was there?

Eva Malin born in 1909 in the Midlands, came to Cuckfield early in 1916, following the death of her father. She and her mother lived at the chauffeur's cottage at Mill Hall with her aunty, Mrs Bell. There was room for them for the duration of the war, as Eva's uncle Mrs Reid's chauffeur, was away at the front.

Her walk to school was through Whiteman's Green, sometimes via Inholmes, in order to visit Mrs Penfold's sweet counter. Eva also recalls the shops in Whiteman's Green, confirming that most of one's everyday needs, meat, bread, groceries etc., were readily available. She remembers the soldiers at the Queen's Hall, often running past them at top speed after hearing the school bell, which gave a ten minute warning of punctuality.

During the dinner hour, a favourite game played with more than a little foreboding, was to visit the graveyard to chase around the chapel. It was said, if you ran round the chapel seven times, a ghost would appear. The children's answer to this horrific possibility was to complete six and three-quarters laps at top speed and then "run for your life". This caution was amply rewarded, for the ghost never appeared.

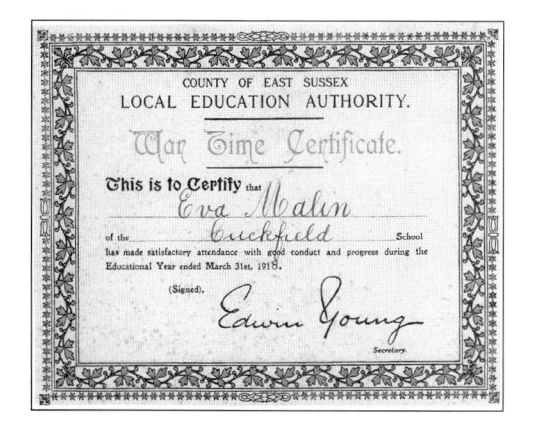

On the way home from school Eva and her friends sometimes stopped at Mrs Godsmark's shop. This was in the front room of the cottage next to the Queen's Hall. Daisy Rhodes remembers the overpowering fumes from Mrs Godsmark's paraffin lamp. This did not however, prevent the children from buying their sweets. They stood on the protruding ledge of bricks beneath the window, and clasping the window-sill, it was possible to look through the window to see what sweets were 'on special offer'. They happily spent the half pennies on 'one of these and one of those'. Eva claims that the children wore down the bricks by standing on them over the many years of the shop's existence. The wear-marks are visible today. Have you seen them?

Another perquisite of the walk home was the sweet chestnut tree at Leyton House (Cuckfield House). Further along the road was the home of Mr B Y Bevan and his family, at Woodcroft, (Manor Drive). Mrs Bevan would have hot soup available for those in need. There were charity boxes of babies clothes etc. She offered goose grease for children with chest problems. It was rubbed on and covered with flannel material.

Tramps visiting the workhouse were quite intimidating for the children. Eva tells of them wending their way across the field footpath from Whiteman's Green. If any of them had any money, they would bury it on the way, retrieving it after their stay. One favourite place to hide money being at the farm gateposts. Such was their impression on the children that none of them dared to go treasure-hunting. In more recent times those with metal detectors have been more successful. Daisy recalls some tramps leaving their money, watches etc. with her grandmother at the shop. It seems the tramps travelled from one workhouse to another doing odd jobs at the farms en route. Any valuables in their possession on entering the workhouse might soon be lost, either to pay for their keep, or stolen by other inmates.

Miss D Dengate now of Handcross used to live in Mayfield House in Ardingly Road, described as 'four doors from the workhouse'. She and her sister were declared to have caught measles from kissing the workhouse children through the railings. She went to school at four years of age. She can particularly remember that each chair had a flower painted on it and hers was a bluebell. Miss Dengate's father was a teacher at Ardingly College and cycled there each day. Before living in Mayfield House the family lived in Walland in London Lane. She well remembers the festivities surrounding the coronation of George V in 1911 and still has the mug presented to all children. She says her mother loved Cuckfield and said that the inhabitants considered the world was *"made up of five continents and Cuckfield"*.

Children playing in the snow at the entrance to Hatchgate Lane.

Fashion in the War

Always ready to play its part in influencing our lives is the fashion scene, good for morale too no doubt. Some of the styles shown here will hopefully interest the reader. The drawings were photographed from the *Mid Sussex Times'* column, "Dress of the Day". Perhaps for some the designs will have helped to brighten the gloom of the time. Anyway it shows us what some people of Mid Sussex may have worn in 1917.

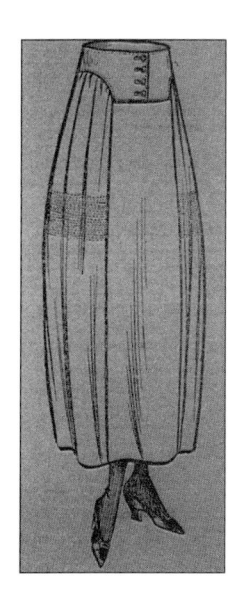

5

JULY - SEPTEMBER 1917

Summer at Home

National Baby Week arrived, and as everywhere it had an impact on Mid Sussex. A National Baby Week Council was formed to "educate the Mother's of the Nation in the care of their children's health and their own."

At an exhibition in London Mrs H B Irving was reputed to have said that it was safer to be a soldier in France than a baby in London. Maybe, but the motivation for the Baby Week was prompted by the enormous numbers of men killed and maimed, fighting. The preservation of the next generation took on a new perspective. All levels of society but particularly the poor were targeted. The *Mid Sussex Times* on July 3rd:

... the idea of National Baby Week has seized upon the imagination of the community as a whole. There can be little doubt that the varied activities of the very influential Council (the National Baby Week Council) primarily responsible for the scheme will do much to efface that black spot upon our civilization, the role of unnecessary and unpreventable child mortality.

– from *Punch Chariviria*

On Friday July 6th Cuckfield, reminiscent of pre-war days, enjoyed a town function at Cuckfield Park. This time it was definitely different, a baby show and fete organised by the Cuckfield Infant Welfare Centre and the Cuckfield Nursing Association. Streams of people were seen making their way to the park to savour the new event in marvellous weather. The committee comprised stalwarts of both churches, namely, Miss Bevan, Miss R Chute Ellis, Mrs Lampson, Mrs Maddock, Miss Payne, Mrs Reid, Mrs Stevens, Mrs M Turner, Miss Turner and Mrs Wilson. Mrs E M Preston the secretary of both the organising institutions performed that role for the show.

The chief item of the day was the baby show. In addition there were marquees housing refreshments, an orchestra, an exhibition of clothing and children's essays. There was a sale of literature appropriate for Baby Week.

The Cuckfield Girl Guides gave displays under the direction of Guide Captain McConnel and Guide Lieutenant Wilson.

The opening ceremony by Mrs Preston addressed the crowd as "Ladies, Gentlemen and Babies", and called upon Lady Glanusk to open the show. Lady Glanusk was of course delighted to perform this task, more especially since it had enabled her to 'come home' for it. Cuckfield Park had indeed been her home. A sister of Captain Charles Warden Sergison, she had lived there until her marriage to Lord Glanusk. Her speech, like all public engagements of the time quickly turned to a patriotic theme. It was claimed, she said, that 50,000 babies a year could be saved if, in the past, heed had been taken of the problems now being addressed. Perhaps, she said, *"we could have put 500,000 more men into the field to help England in its hour of need. The Baby Week movement was therefore one of vital importance."* This said, Lady Glanusk declared the Baby Show open.

A silver bowl for the best Cuckfield Infant Welfare Centre baby, with other prizes in the two classes for infants, was on offer. Consolation gifts were presented to all entries. The judge for the competition was Dr Esther Carling. There was a system of scoring based upon the weight, cleanliness, clothing, general condition (skin and physique) and appearance of the competitors. Reggie Rapley won the Challenge Bowl.

Results – Babies under 12 months - 1st. Robert Ellis. 2nd. James Ridley.

Babies 12 mnths/2 years – 1st. Reginald Rapley. 2nd. Alice Mansbridge.

Best turned out Pram (with baby). – 1st. Mrs Cleaver. 2nd. Mrs Rist.

Makeshift garment for children – 1st. Mrs E Selby. 2nd. Mrs Turner.

In a separate competition judged by Mrs B Y Bevan, an essay by school children, entitled "If Mother was away all day how would I feed and take care of baby".

Group One - 1st. May Redwood. 2nd. Norah Tidey. 3rd. Mabel Voller.

Group Two -1st. Gladys Quin. 2nd. Olive Flint. 3rd. Violet Quin.

Finally responding to a vote of thanks Dr Carling congratulated Cuckfield on its exhibition and wished the Welfare Centre well. She said she hoped National Baby Week and its aftermath would help to improve the future and that nothing would stop the establishment of a Ministry of Public Health.

News of the many Baby Week activities in the towns and villages of Mid Sussex featured prominently in the *Mid Sussex Times*. In the July 10th issue from the Notes and Comments column, the views of almost certainly a middle-aged male reporter:

> Balcombe, Cuckfield and Lindfield had their baby days last week and in each locality some specially fine children came before the judges. With the introduction now of Welfare Centres springing up all over the country babies should have a better chance, because their mothers are being instructed in the matter of caring for them. We have heard of infants being given whelks to eat and sausages and have seen them sucking candles, no attempt made to take them from them. Then

mothers wonder why their children never seem to thrive, the ignorance of some mothers in one way is surprising and in another way is not. A girl gets married and a baby comes along, she has no experience perhaps in looking after a child, has never washed or clothed one, she is like a mariner without a compass, she does not know her bearings. If there is an Infant Welfare Centre or a Mothers and Babies Club in their town or village it is easy for her to gain instruction and advice. The well-to-do who give whatever aid they can to starting and maintaining these organisations are rendering a good service to their country.

In the same newspaper, came details of another successful concert at the Cuckfield VAD Hospital held on July 3rd. The hospital, the Queen's Hall, was the venue for the evening. Presumably space was made by pushing the beds back to the walls. A large party of soldiers undergoing treatment at the Cottage Hospital in Haywards Heath were invited. Some patients in Cuckfield acted and sang in the concert with the locals making the show a big success. These concerts were now a feature of local entertainment.

The Reverend S Maddock used the National Baby Week theme when making observations during a sermon. He drew attention to the lack of a playing field or recreation ground in Cuckfield. It is strange he said that a town of the public spirit and wealth of Cuckfield should have golf links but no public cricket ground. Mothers in the town had said to him that the children were forbidden to play in the streets and they must not trespass in the fields. London boys have better facilities for cricket and other field games than many towns and villages in Mid Sussex.

On July 4th Cuckfield school recognised the 141st anniversary of American independence. The Stars and Stripes were hoisted on the flag pole. Mr Herrington, the headmaster, had some years before visited the United States and had been influenced by the patriotism shown in the schools. He claimed that no other school in Britain would be making such a grand occasion of this day as Cuckfield. The celebrations may have been postponed due to the bad weather but for the presence of several American ladies anxious to witness the rather elaborately planned ceremony. Mr Herrington made a carefully prepared address. Speaking to the flag, he referred to his pupils as, children of the Motherland, of Sussex and of Cuckfield, *"we greet, welcome and salute thee"*. American hymns were sung, as well as, *"Yankee Doodle"*, *"South Carolina"*, *"Marching through Georgia"* and even *"Uncle Ned"*. Certainly impressive. Mr Herrington was a keen supporter of America. His enthusiasm for their patriotism was a feature on Empire Day..

Relatives had more news of Cuckfield servicemen. Two more deaths, George Murrell died as a prisoner of war, Mrs Murrell had heard that he had been taken a prisoner on New Year's day. Alfred Pennefold was killed in action on June 16th. Mrs Pennefold had four sons, three were in the army and a twelve-year old was at home. On a more cheerful note, Frank Knight was promoted to Chief Motor Mechanic in the Royal Naval Motor Boat Reserve. Before joining up he worked for Denman's in Broad Street.

The progress of war in France and Belgium was always in the news, as were the now regular bombing raids over London and the South East. Nevertheless, never forgotten were the other theatres of war. Cuckfield's sons were also serving in Egypt, Mesopotamia and on the seas. A letter from Private Bone from Egypt in June had news of some Cuckfieldians. In February there was a "Letter from Mesopotamia" from Corporal Mitchell. He turned scribe again with another received in July. This time entitled "Life in Baghdad". Some extracts of his letter are:

> At last after weeks of trekking we are settled down, and hope to stop here for the summer. We have just received an accumulated mail of some weeks, and I received altogether nine letters and a parcel of January 13th. It is fine to get mail again, and I daresay they will come regularly now that things have settled down . . . I managed to get a pass into the city with some more fellows. We were very disappointed with the place. The streets were narrow and dirty and there was nothing at all in the bazaars. But since then things have changed tremendously. The bazaars are open and full of stuff. Heaven only knows were they get it all from! Restaurants have sprung up, where you can get quite a decent feed, and I even managed to get an ice in one place. The people crowd the streets and the women wear the most gawdy apparel. . . . Our tent is situated in a palm grove close to the river. The trees make nice shade. I have had to go out on another stunt at an hour's notice. We were going for a fortnight, but after four days we had used up all our wire, so had to return It was only a small column and our job was strafing Arabs. We smashed up two lots and captured their sheep, and it fell to us to drive them back to Baghdad. The officer put me in charge, gave me twenty men and told me to carry on. We left at 4.30am and got to Baghdad at 5.30pm. I had to do the cowboy business of galloping after the stray ones. About a hundred died from exhaustion. The heat is 110 in the shade as I write. It is getting too hot for the flies, they are dying off. A canteen has been opened in Baghdad, now we can get a few extras. I am trying to learn Hindustani, I have been put in charge of a horse line, all the drivers are Indian. Feel a bit tired this morning (May 16th). Had a fifty mile ride in the desert yesterday, repairing wire.

While readers of the *Mid Sussex Times* were enjoying that letter, there was sad news of Lance Corporal Bowell of Whiteman's Green. He died of heatstroke in Basra on July 22nd. He had been wounded in Flanders in 1915, then returned to duty when fit. Cecil Bowell was with the force that captured Baghdad, where he was wounded again. A colleague of Corporal Mitchell perhaps? Albert Chinnery, a sapper with the Royal Engineers, serving as a waiter in the Officer's Mess was killed when a shell hit the house. Mrs Mitchell of Albany Villas heard that her son William, with the Middlesex Regiment was killed. Her second son lost in the war.

A meeting of the Urban District Council resolved that Mr Hubert Bates be appointed as the local representative of the Food Production Department. He was a member of the council and a keen horticulturist.

Mr Herrington received a letter from the United States Ambassador congratulating the school's celebration of July 4th.

Bradley and Vaughan, Estate Agents, placed an advert in the *Mid Sussex Times* on July 24th. It said, *"Unprecedented demand for furnished houses in Mid Sussex (Owing so far) to the immunity of air raids. We will be pleased to hear from house owners wishing to rent"*.

On July 26th sixty children from London arrived in Cuckfield and Lindfield for two weeks holiday. They came under the auspices of the Children's Country Holiday's Fund. At the end of their stay a further batch would take their place. There were some amusing tales of the childrens' food preferences. One little boy claimed to like London eggs rather than fresh ones and another preferred London milk because it came from a shop with a marble counter. It was cleaner than *"getting the milk in a jug from a dirty cow, it comes from down under there where a woman pulls the tassels"*.

On the wet morning of August 4th the people of Mid Sussex awoke to the Great Anniversary. That Saturday marked the starting of the fourth year of the war. On the previous Tuesday readers of the *Mid Sussex Times* will have read the leader article:

> No great war, be it remembered, has ever left a nation just as it found it. And when this conflict is over we shall see a changed England. The young generation will change the most . . . It may be written in the stars that our children may have all our work to do again for the good of their souls. That is what it makes it so irritating to hear this conflict called Armageddon. Armageddon is not merely a war of all the nations; it is the ultimate battle. This is not going to be the last war, and those who expect it to be so are only preparing themselves for disappointment. As long as the world and human nature last there will be the appeal of the sword, and it will be necessary until the end of time, in our humble judgement, for the nations who want peace to prepare for war.

On that Saturday the Central Committee for National Patriotic Organisations sponsored the idea of meetings held throughout the Empire to mark the third anniversary of the outbreak of war. Several gatherings were organised in Mid Sussex, four of them, took place in Haywards Heath, Burgess Hill, Hurstpierpoint and Cuckfield. The time of the country-wide meetings was 7.30pm, and a common resolution had been prepared that would be presented to the gathered assembly, reaffirming the nation's commitment to its war ideals.

Haywards Heath's public meeting was at the Corn Exchange. The person moving the resolution, was Major A H C Kenney-Herbert of Cuckfield, his words echoed throughout the land. *"That, on this, the third anniversary of the declaration of a righteous war, this meeting of the citizens of Haywards Heath, records its inflexible determination to continue to a victorious end, the struggle in maintenance of those ideals of liberty and justice which are the common and sacred cause of the Allies."* Major Kenney-Herbert then went on to give a stirring view of the war to date. His address became increasingly passionate, showing no feeling for the difference between the military, the politician or the ordinary citizen. *"Don't forget what the Germans have done. See that your foot is on his neck, and keep it there, but never make a friend of a German again."* He ended on a religious note. *"It is our privilege to take this matter of the war to the Throne of Almighty God. I feel that the nation has not sufficiently interceded before His throne for the victory we rightly believe we deserve. The German cup of iniquity must be filled by now, and we ask God to make Germany drink it."*

Burgess Hill held its meeting in the open air on land next to Barclay's Bank. It was the chairman of the meeting, Mr A B Taylor, the chairman of the Burgess Hill Urban District Council who proposed the resolution.

Hurstpierpoint's meeting was in the Drill Hall. The chairman for the meeting was Colonel W H Campion, who had fought in the Crimea (1854-56). Admiral Sir Lewis Beaumont proposed the resolution.

Cuckfield, different from the others, recognised the event in the way that it knew best. That was, a service of Thanksgiving in the evening, at the designated time, in the parish church. Before that, at noon, the Peace Bell sounded with a prayer for victory and peace. As usual the church was filled. The Cuckfield Volunteers, the Girl Guides and Boy Scouts were well represented, and the Crosses of St George and the Union Jack were in evidence. At least a fifth of Cuckfield's population heard the Reverend Gerrard Hutton from Brighton deliver his sermon, exhorting his listeners to the righteousness of "our cause". He said *"Looking back, we had to thank God that England, although not knowing then that the enemy had this country as its objective, had not hesitated to enter the war on behalf of righteousness, justice and freedom."*

The Volunteers' Platoon Commander, B Y Bevan proposed the national resolution. He altered it to read, *". . . inflexible determination to continue, under Divine Providence, to a victorious end, . . . "*. The whole congregation rose to its feet in assent.

At all the meetings the resolutions, were of course seconded and enthusiastically and comprehensively, carried. As we've learnt it was events such as these, where so many people gathered, that the preachers and speakers could deliver stirring homilies to patriotism. Probably important was the morale boosting that must have given strength to "those at home". Without the mass media we now take for granted, word of mouth was the most effective way of carrying the population forward. The parish church was certainly the centre of the rural community if not quite the same in the cities.

The VAD Hospital in the Queen's Hall was full of patients, servicemen, receiving recuperative treatment before returning to fight. The townspeople had started making regular gifts of food to supplement the patients' rations. So organised had it become that by August a thank-you note was appearing fortnightly in the *Mid Sussex Times*. The contributors were named together with details of the various gifts. As well as fruit and vegetables where it all started, eggs, cakes, butter, jam, books and even pyjamas were given. What with the patients taking part in the entertainment programme of concerts, the hospital could truly be regarded as part of the community.

Such had become the worry over food production and availability that the Government had introduced a policy that Local Authorities including District Councils would appoint Food Committees. These should consist of no more than twelve members, some of whom were to be co-opted and must include one woman and one representative of labour. Cuckfield Urban District Council held a special meeting on August 16th to select its committee. From the council Messrs A Beeching, H Bates (already the local rep of the Food Production Dept) and J Denman. Another recommended was Miss K Caffyn and either Mr Bowell or Mr Gibson, the former declined. The first item to be considered was sugar distribution. The food committee had the powers to register grocers and other retailers of sugar. October 1st was the last day for registration without which no retailer could deal in sugar. Other foodstuffs including bread and meat would follow. The local committee would be expected to enforce the Food Controller's (Lord Rhondda) price fixing regulations.

A serious sign of the forthcoming food rationing, resisted for so long, was the notice produced by Cuckfield's International Stores. It said that:

1. After December 30th 1917, sugar will be distributed to the public, in accordance with the rules applied by the Food Controller.
2. A card will be issued to each householder by the Local Food Committee, and supplies will only be obtainable by the holders of such cards.
3. Application for the Sugar Card must be made on a form that will be issued through the Postal Authorities during September.

> The unrestricted German submarine warfare brought Britain close to starvation rations in the spring of 1917. This news was largely kept from the public. Beer and confectionery supplies were cut in June and price limits put on basic goods in August. Coal rationing started in November. The Government appealed for reduced consumption, but in February 1918 meat and fats were rationed in London. By July, full ration books for all meat and dairy products, were introduced.

In the *Mid Sussex Times* of August 14th in the column 'Up and Down the County' the following ironic piece appeared:

> It will be news to many in Cuckfield that there is a Volunteer Fire Brigade in the town, and 400 feet of hose. The firemen are members of the Sussex Volunteer Regiment, and they have put in a good deal of time this summer practising hose drill. Whenever an outbreak of fire occurs the men to get in touch with are Corporal Carter of South Street and Mr Croucher (Council Surveyor) of Glebe Road. Some day Cuckfield may rise to a fire engine and an escape and purchase a lot more hose. The inhabitants of the larger houses will then feel a little more

secure. At present, however, they are not supposed to meet trouble half way. "Let's have a big blaze first, and then we'll see about a fire engine and an escape." That is how the question is viewed today.

In the same paper, it was noted that, up to August 14th the Roll of Honour in Mid Sussex had revealed that 450 men had been killed from the twenty one parishes listed. At that same date Cuckfield had lost 49 of those.

More news came of Captain Reid of Mill Hall with the *London Gazette* publishing the official announcement of the award of his Military Cross. It said that he *"showed conspicuous gallantry and devotion to duty. He led his company with great judgement and coolness under heavy fire. By his skilful use of his Lewis Gun he prevented a counter attack on his exposed flank, having appreciated the danger at the right moment".*

Other awards for bravery announced around this time were Sgt Leonard Palmer, (Lodge Farm) the Distinguished Conduct Medal. Sgt Major Rhodes received a Serbian decoration for gallant service in that country and Sgt A Selby, the Military Medal fighting at Pozieres.

The second huge offensive of 1917 started on July 31st in Flanders, the Third Battle of Ypres. There was heavy rain in Flanders. The battles were reported in the press and at home news was awaited. Names of wounded soldiers came. 2nd Lt Douglas Wood, Royal Berkshire Regiment was hit in the thigh by a bullet "going over the top". Private T Markwick, Royal West Kents was wounded while acting as a stretcher bearer. Private John Young, Royal Sussex Regiment, hit in both legs by shrapnel.

The town's gas supply came under threat when one of the two stokers applied for exemption from service. The Local Tribunal met to consider the matter. The stoker was lame from birth and was classified C2. He had been discharged from the army in 1916, after three months service, as medically unfit. The tribunal granted him conditional exemption, which meant that he may need to apply again. Technically, only those classified in the A category could be sent abroad, Bs and Cs filling the "home postings". Malingerers beware!

Percy Reeve of the Machine Gun Corps, a Cuckfield barber, having served seven months in France, was back in an English hospital suffering from rheumatic fever. His wife Nellie had taken over the shop when Percy joined the army in 1916. She had retained all her husbands' shaving customers still left in Cuckfield. When asked on whom did she first practice shaving, she replied, *"Percy of course!"*.

There was a sad story reported in Haywards Heath Magistrates Court on August 27th. William Bates aged, 73 was charged with stealing two marrows from the schoolboys' garden at Cuckfield school. He admitted taking them. In June he was bound over for six months charged with stealing three broccoli from some allotments in the town. Mr Bates had been remanded in Maidstone Gaol for a week, awaiting a doctor's report on the state of his mind. The prison doctor declared that the defendant was senile, very deaf and rather dull of intellect. Nevertheless, in his opinion, Mr Bates was responsible for his actions. He was sentenced to fourteen days imprisonment. Rough justice?

THE DITTY BOX

During the many days of working on a book, the ambition of all researchers is to find something special, an incident or episode, which makes the narrative special. It may be of historic importance, it may be funny. Or, in the case that follows, a personal story to touch the heart. It adds poignancy and must be told. It uncovers a story that is the stuff of fiction.

In looking for individual stories from the older members of the town, and hoping for some first hand tales of their families, during 1917, the well-known Old Cuckfieldian Tom Wells, revealed his uncle's ditty box. This uncle, George Botting served with the Royal Marines Light Infantry. He carried with him as part of his kit a wooden box in which he kept his personal odds and ends including letters etc. After opening the ditty box and examining its many contents a path of research followed. The *Mid Sussex Times*, the *Parish Magazine* and the Royal Marines Museum revealed the story. A moving account unfolded of a young married couple during the summer of 1917. Such then is the story of George and May Botting.

George Botting and Dora May Wells were married on February 9th 1916 at Holy Trinity Church and their home was at 4 Jubilee Cottages in Broad Street. Before registering for military service in December 1915, George was a nurseryman at Charlesworth Orchids in Haywards Heath. He played football for Cuckfield Football Club, which won the Mid-Sussex Junior League in 1907-08. He was also an athlete with Haywards Heath Athletic Club and won many prizes. May was a dressmaker. Below are Jubilee Cottages featured on the front of a postcard sent to George while serving in Dorset in 1916.

George served with the Royal Marines Light Infantry in Dorset, Kent and then France. He kept a diary and entries made follow, interspersed with extracts of May's letters to him.

June 17th – Sent my small diary and a few souvenirs home by a chum going on leave. Weather still very warm.
June 18th – Anxiously awaiting news from May, no letter for over a week. Still drilling and training for open warfare.
June 20th – Birthday card from May, I wonder why no letter - beginning to feel worried about her.

May's card dated June 15th, *"Just a card to wish you many, many happy returns. Hope this will reach you in time. So anxiously waiting a letter. No line, nothing for a fortnight."* How important letters were.

June 21st – Card and book from Sybil and a letter from Mother. Met Joe in the evening and to celebrate my birthday had a bottle of champagne which put us in the best of spirits, only missing was a letter from the "Kid".
June 22nd – On the move to Bullecourt a village close by and to the south of Arras, went into Beaurais on the ground that was once in Fritz's hands.
June 23rd – Done nothing this day but fell in at 9.00pm for night digging a communication trench just behind the support area, the village of Gavrelle. Had the good luck to be tolled off as we fell in, with nineteen others for day work, so fell out that night.
June 24th – Fell in at 5.30am and after a walk of 4 miles over the open and through trenches reached our job close to Gavrelle, clearing a trench for stretchers only. Very risky job in daylight.
June 26th – A parcel and letter from May - most pleased with letter and to know she is getting my letters alright.
June 27th Rumours of a big attack on Oppy Wood by our people.
June 28th – No attack this morning but may come off at any time. Had a stand off today so they gave us the luxury of a good bath and we can do with it this warm weather. Our barrage opened at about 8 o'clock. A Yorkshire Brigade went over and took Oppy Wood with very few casualties, saw some prisoners in a "cage" close by our camp.
Sunday July 1st – No work today, a short service from our C O. Going into Arras for a look around this afternoon.
July 2nd – Work on the railway in the morning getting home about twelve o'clock. Parade in the afternoon and the C O warned us to get a good stock of cigs as we move up the line on Tuesday for a week or two.
July 3rd – Feeling rather shaky, an abscess on shoulder troubling me a lot - went to have it dressed. Doctor sent me away to the Field Ambulance at Moelincourt.
July 4th – Sent on to CMS at Croivres which was a large rest station, where I found my old friend the wire netting bed, not at all bad if the wire is round.
July 5th – Nothing to do but see the doctor in the morning and then

read and sleep all day.

July 6th – The band of the East Yorks gave us a tune in the afternoon. Quite a treat to get my meals fairly decent on a plate after using a canteen for everything for six months.

July 11th – A wet morning, feel sorry for my mates up the line, up to their knees in water and mud.

July 15th – Rejoined the Battalion out resting in the cutting on the Arras - Lens line.

July 19th – Met my old pal Jack Wilkinson in my company just back from Blighty where he had been with trench foot. Sorry to find my mail had all been sent back home again.

(Trench foot was a fungal infection of the feet caused by cold, wet and insanitary conditions, it could turn gangrenous and result in amputation).

July 20th – Letter from May, first for three weeks, pleased to get it.

July 23rd – After three days easy time when I went to Arras again - a splendid city before the war but now knocked about terribly. We moved up the line occupying the front line to the left of Gavrelle. My post being just in front of the now famous windmill of which but a very few bricks and bits of timber remain. Had a very quiet week in the line especially at our part which being only 60 yards from Fritz he was afraid to shell us for fear of hitting his own men. I made some splendid canteens of tea and no one can realise unless they have been out here how nice it goes down about 5 o'clock in the morning after being on watch and working all night. Watch on the parapet is very trying at times as every tuft of grass or bush seems to conceal a Bosche and with bullets whizzing and lights going up all around it is a very weird sight.

July 31st – Got relieved about midnight and after a trying tramp over muddy ground during which I managed to fall in two shell holes we eventually reached the camp allotted to us at daybreak.

(On that day the 3rd Battle of Ypres started. Also known as Passchendaele it was the last great battle of attrition).

Aug 1st – Spent the day cleaning up ourselves and gear, which needless to say we badly needed.

Aug 2nd – Warned off to get ready to go to XIII Corps Draft Training Depot as an instructor to the new draft for our Battalion - given my L/Cpls stripe dating from April. Saw Joe in the evening.

Aug 3rd – With two more NCOs went by lorry to Couchez a la Tour and found we had struck lucky having a nice room at the Maire's home to have meals and do our writing and a nice place to sleep in.

Aug 4th – A wet day but cleared up enough to make us go to the training ground.

> Aug 5th – The whole depot went on a route march which did not worry me as I only wore belt and bayonet. New draft arrived so have plenty of writing and running about to do. A special service in the evening to commemorate the third anniversary of the war.
> Aug 6th – Started with squad training in earnest and find we've got our work cut out to teach them discipline as they do not seem to realise the importance of it.
> Aug 7th – Settling down to job quite nicely and picking up a lot of information respecting drill and gaining confidence without which it is useless trying to drill a squad.

May's next letter, saved in the box, dated August 7th, *"I don't think I have much to write about this time, as I am anxiously waiting another from you to say if you have gone to your new job and how you like it. Is it bombing? Are you still bomber with the Batt. We have actually had two fine sunny days and talk about holiday people, we are swamped with them here."* (The letter goes on for a few pages but then it ends), *"Wednesday morning. Just got your letter, so glad."* . . .

> Aug 8th – Weather improving and spirits rise.
> Aug 9th, 10th, 11th – Training.
> Aug 12th – Sunday, nothing doing in the training line so went into town and had photo taken, 6 of us, happy days.
> Aug 13th, 14th – Training, getting on very well with my squad and getting them quite smart

From May dated August 14th, *"It was a great relief to get your letter written 6th this morning 8 days coming. Some time for a green envelope wasn't it? The envelope inside was torn did you do that, if not it had been opened, the outside one looked like it too, but nothing was crossed out. I am so glad you are comfortable, Boy, make the most of it while you can. I hope to goodness you will be able to manage it, and will stay there for 2 months, it's something to know you are safe."* (May had been suffering with a very bad throat problem for some months by this time, she goes on) *"Yesterday I made much more sound, it seemed as though I was hoarse with a cold, today its not so strong again, but there's a voice somewhere . . . The weather in France seems just like ours, it seems the summer has gone doesn't it? Its quite chilly, if you don't get vests this winter let me know, no going without mind!"* . . .

> Aug 15th – Got our photos back and cannot say they flatter us, but not too bad.
> Aug 16th – Weather lovely and warm and all the farmers very busy harvesting, mostly women and old men working though, very few young men about excepting the miners, we being in the centre of a large mining district.

From May dated August 16th, *"What a lovely long letter I had from you yesterday written 8th and 9th. Thanks so much, by that I can see you are pleased with yourself Boy and happier, it must be nice to be in civilisation once more, lets hope you stay there. I feel more contented over you than I've done since you've been out, fancy 8 months. So glad you are getting on with your drilling, you must be pretty good to have been picked. I don't think I shall live in France if you have to work so hard, can you imagine me milking 12 cows, like your lady, but what about coming and staying with you for my summer holiday, sounds alright doesn't it? I am wondering how your sports went off and if you ran, it must seem like old times for you Boy . . . The guns have been awful this morning. The windows are chattering away with the guns. . ."* (The letter goes on with family and local news, her throat is improving, the tone is happy. He asks for a shirt), *"yes you shall have one. I expect it is for evening wear now you swank with the mayor. . . . Hope you will like the snap enclosed, it's very good but Mum looks so old. Fancy it hardly seems possible does it, we have been married 18 months. Can you get your photo taken Darling now? . . ."*

Note, the guns in France could be heard and felt in Mid Sussex!

The Royal Naval Division was formed in 1913. Winston Churchill, First Lord of the Admiralty, foresaw that in case of war the Navy would have a surplus of men available for the ships of the Fleet. The much smaller professional Army would require all the trained men available. Thus, three brigades were made ready to fight on the land. One composed of Marines and the other two from the Royal Naval Volunteer Reserve and the Royal Fleet Reserve. The Royal Marines Light Infantry became a separate division from the Royal Marine Artillery in 1855, during the Crimean War, for administrative reasons. In 1923 the two became one again.

Within the Royal Marines Brigade was the 2nd Battalion, in which George Botting served. The Brigade took part in the Arras Offensive in April 1917. Its main objectives were, the capture of the village of Gavrelle, and the Gavrelle Windmill. This latter action was the Battle of Arleux. The windmill was captured on April 28th with heavy casualties. Many marines were taken prisoner when they streamed through the only gap in the barbed wire and were cut off. Of course there were many acts of bravery, resulting in the award of one Military Cross, one Distinguished Conduct Medal and several Military Medals.

Having captured both objectives, the 1st and 2nd RMLI Battalions remained in the sector until August, manning the trenches alternately. This meant four days in the front line, three in support, followed by three more in the front and then back to the reserve position. The main Arras Offensive was abandoned on May 17th, but, as always the localised fighting continued.

On August 17th George Botting's battalion retired to Frevillers for training. George, however, had already taken up his duties as an instructor.

> Aug 17th, 18th – Nothing to report.
> Aug 19th – Feeling a bit groggy with a touch of dysentry I think but manage to keep going.
> Aug 20th – Day of rest. Go to Auchel in the evening for a walk, quite a nice place, actually boasting a bazaar after our style. Buy a pocket wallet for a photo of the best little Girl in the World.

That was the last entry made in the diary. On August 23rd tragedy struck. George Botting was not to be killed in action, in the trenches, from gas or even illness but by accident. He was following his duties as an instructor, when, on the grenade practice ground the worst possible drama happened.

May Botting received the following letter from Lieutenant Colonel R C Hawkins:

> I very much regret having to send you the sad news of the death of your husband, Lance Corporal G E Botting, who was killed on the 23rd August in a bombing accident. He was struck through the heart and died instantly. Fortunately he did not suffer any pain, and I honestly believe he knew nothing of the accident. Your husband was a magnificent instructor, and was much admired and loved by his men. He was carrying out his duty on the morning of the accident, and was instructing men in how to throw live grenades. All precautions possible were taken, but the accident occured through a premature exploding in the recruit's hand, causing the death of your husband and serious injuries to two other men. He was buried in the British Cemetery at ———, where his grave could be seen if you visit the area after the war. I am deeply distressed at the accident, and the loss of Lance Corporal Botting is severely felt. Please accept my deepest sympathy.

Other officers wrote letters of sympathy to the widow and Captain Edwards sent one to George's mother in Pentland Road, Haywards Heath. It can only be imagined, that receiving such letters, loved ones could gain some strength from them. Those, who had the thankless task of writing the countless number required during the war, would have hoped that the recipients were comforted by the knowledge that their husband or son was not forced to suffer, and that death came quickly. Exactly how much detail of the nature of the death that the family needed or wanted to know is so very difficult to understand. Captain Edwards told Mrs Botting:

> I can scarcely express my deep sympathy for you in your sorrow . . .. Lance Corporal Botting was teaching a recruit how to throw bombs. The recruit took the bomb in his hand to throw it and it exploded prematurely. A small piece entered your son's body just over the heart, and he died practically instantaneously and without pain. The man who threw the bomb and a Sergeant Instructor were also wounded, I fear, fatally. As belonging to the same Battalion as your son, and sharing many dangers with him, I should like to express my admiration for him as a thoroughly efficient and courageous man, and I should like you to know how popular he was with all his comrades. The Battalion never had a finer man and many of us have lost a dear friend.

May was sent the ditty box from France. It has stayed with family ever since. In it are letters from May to George, a pipe, a case with two cigarettes, a wallet encasing May's photograph, (see over) military handbooks and of course the diary. May's last letter to George written on August 16th was a particularly happy one, expressing the belief that his present job away from the trenches must be safe, and that she hoped he would keep it for as long as possible. The unfeelingness of the war and the detachment of authority, manifested itself some days after the terrible news when the box arrived back in England. The box was addressed to Haywards Heath railway station and that it was to be collected. There was obviously no money in the budget to ease the pain of a grieving widow. Searching the box to write this story was a very harrowing experience. May never remarried, she looked after her mother, who died aged 100 years.

The Ditty Box.

In the foreground is the diary, a packet of shampoo powder leaning against some shaving soap, a pipe and a cigarette case with two cigarettes from 1917. Also shown are greetings' cards, a Royal Marine's hat badge, a national registration card enclosing a lock of May's hair, a military manual and tucked in the lid, George's last letter from May.

The Royal Marines Roll of Honour shows that:
In Lapugndy Military Cemetery, France.
BOTTING George Ernest, L/Cpl PO 1451,
lies in plot V, row D, grave 14.

A SMALL TOWN AT WAR

79

HOW DO I LOVE THEE - Wilfred Owen. M.C.

I cannot woo thee as the lion his mate,
With proud parade and fierce prestige of presence;
Nor thy fleet fancy may I captivate
With pastoral attitudes in flowery pleasance;
Nor will I kneeling court thee with sedate
And comfortable plans of husbandhood;
Nor file before thee as a candidate....
I cannot woo thee as a lover would.

To wrest thy hand from rivals, iron gloved,
Or cheat them by a craft, I am not clever.
But I do love thee even as Shakespeare loved,
Most gently wild, and desperately for ever,
Full-hearted, grave, and manfully in vain,
With thought, high pain, and ever vaster pain.

THE MEMORIAL SERVICE

Cuckfield town was in the news again on September 4th. The feature was a huge memorial service at the parish church to honour those who had died since the last one held in February. On that occasion eight men were remembered, this time, fourteen. So large was the congregation that extra chairs were needed, even then many had to stand. Therefore, many hundreds of people including numbers from outside Cuckfield attended. It was in such gatherings that the townsfolk could express their feelings, their unity with their neighbours, and to draw strength in such trying times. Recording this important event from the writings of the day helps to understand our predecessors a little better. From the *Mid Sussex Times*:

> The old world town of Cuckfield is intensely patriotic. A very large number of her sons are with the Forces, and up to present there are upon the town's Roll of Honour fifty names. Periodically the Vicar (Canon Wilson) a dear, good priest, whom all the Boys love, holds a memorial service at the Parish Church, and to it the inhabitants flock, as well as persons from other parishes who like to pay a tribute of respect in God's House to the memory of gallant friends. The memorial service last Sunday evening was specially for men with Cuckfield associations who have recently made the supreme sacrifice:- James Attree, Cecil Bowell, George Botting, Albert Chinnery, Ellis Dancy, Thomas Henley, Arthur Holden, W Holford Mitchell, W H Mitchell, George Murrell, James Ridley, Alfred Pennefold, Harcourt Turner, Charles Tincler. (Another eight were to die by the end of the year).

The service was full of ceremony. The Volunteers, the Scouts and the Guides were well represented. There was a processional hymn, Mr W Herrington the cross bearer and choristers William Clarke and Charles Philpott carried the Union Jack and the Cross of St George. Each flag was adorned by a crape knot.

> Platoon Commander B Y Bevan, with striking emphasis, read a special lesson from Revelations xxi, "And I saw a new heaven and a new earth . . . And God shall wipe away all tears from their eyes; and there shall be no more death, neither sorrow, nor crying, neither shall their be any more pain". The sermon was preached by the Reverend R H C Mertons, and it might well be entitled "Recognition beyond the Grave". The text was, "Let us pass over onto the other side" . . . The reverend gentleman asked the sorrowing ones not to dwell on the past, but to look at the future. Questions naturally arose as to the departed. Where were they, what were they like, what were they doing, did they remember their loved ones? . . .."
> (Before the evening ended, after the National Anthem, the organist Mr Attewell played the "Dead March from Saul"). A hush fell upon the congregation when the organ ceased. And the stillness, which could be felt, was broken by Sergeant Bugler Hounsell and Bugler L Burtenshaw sounding, from the west door of the church, "The Last Post", the gripping pathos of which brought tears to many eyes. The congregation knew the service had ended. As some of them wended their way homewards they were not unmindful of the fact that the security of the living had been won by the sacrifice of the dead.

Consider then, there would have been several hundred people at the service, Cuckfield's population was in the order of 1,850. Over three hundred men were serving in the forces at this time (more than 400 served over the four years). Given that a number attended from outside the town, the scale of the event and the effect upon the town must have been quite staggering. What were the young widows and parents feelings? Did they believe in the centuries old commandment that dying for your country was glorious? It may have been unavoidable, even necessary in the eyes of some, but always unacceptable to those at home. But, after the trauma of such a high profile church service, what were they really thinking? The sermon, the lesson, the tragic music, followed by the "Last Post" would have almost been the last straw. However, life for our forebears eighty-two years ago was not as sophisticated as ours today, nor were life's expectations as high. Compared to life in the second half of the twentieth century the Great War happened in a largely static environment. The class system predominated. The war's impact on society was enormous. The romantic and accepted view that men knew best and women were to be protected would soon be a thing of the past. It would not be long before the ordinary person would look beyond their confining boundaries for a future. The fortitude shown by them during the war years was marvellous.

So, what were their thoughts as they left church that September day?

Where was the glory? Were the ideals of the politicians the ideals of those whose loved ones would not return? They may have been thinking that, they and their lost husbands, sons and sweethearts did not understand the real implications of war. This being particularly so at the beginning, and now finally, innocence was lost. When would the killing stop?

ENTRENCHED IN INNOCENCE
– Gabrielle Whyte

Never again will such unblemished innocence be seen,
Weaned on the abstractness of honour and glory
The beginning of this war was palpably innocent,
Smiling, achingly, youthful images.... lambs to the slaughter
Who all but solicited their own downfall with sweet generosity,
Not a trace of cynicism etched on their faces
Guilelessness beyond our comprehension
Romantic introspection irrecoverably lost.

THE SUMMER STORM

In the chapter on the Spring Offensive we saw that the time was fast approaching for another major British attack on the Western Front. Preparations to 'end the war' were under way!

On July 6th the Arab revolutionary forces captured Aqaba from the Turks, making it into the centre for British logistics support for the Arab revolt in the north. This was one of the famous, Lawrence of Arabia's moves, which played an important part in the Arabian campaigns against 300 years of rule by the Ottoman Empire.

The German Chancellor, Bethman Hollweg resigned on July 14th. This followed the collapse of a socialist and centre party's peace declaration in the German parliament.

Following the abdication of King Constantine of Greece, King George V renounced all German titles, and then changed the family names. The House of Hanover became Windsor and Battenberg translated to Mountbatten. This enhanced the status and reputation of the Royal Family. In the early months of the war all aliens were ruthlessly investigated. Some were interned, though innocent, while others were persecuted. People with German or Austrian sounding names had a particularly hard time.

On the Eastern Front the fighting continued with the final Russian offensive in Galacia (Poland). The Austro-German counter attack started on

July 15th and by August 15th had effectively neutralised the Russian effort.

On July 31st the much awaited British offensive at Ypres began. As previously described it was Field Marshal Haig's plan to push the Germans out of France and Belgium.

It may be worth dwelling on the perceived importance of this, the Third Battle of Ypres. The British High Command had long held the belief, following the failed attempt of a mobile war in 1914, the successful side would be the one able to win a war of attrition. The philosophy of the British Army was to prosecute huge offensives, wear down the enemy and then make the final definitive push. In 1915 the first such venture to eliminate the phenomenon of trench warfare and return the initiative to the attacker was the Allied Champagne and Artois-Loos campaign. The result of which, was a large number of casualties and ultimate failure. In 1916 the fateful Somme Offensive was 'the big one', more failure with even more casualties. In two years of all out war no significant gain of territory was evident. The plans of 1917 had been severely compromised by the failure of the French at Aisne. Also, the British campaign at Arras had produced no real success. Thus, the manifestly vital breakout at Ypres was so necessary to make an end to the stalemate. Not only did the army need some real success but so did the politicians back home. Therefore, all hopes rested on the Third Battle of Ypres to secure that break through.

The British Army's morale was high following the Battle of Messines in June. From around July 16th until the 25th a huge artillery bombardment was mounted. 3,000 guns fired over four million shells on the German positions. There was no shortage of ordnance now. Some detail in this war always seemed to get overlooked. This huge concentration of explosives caused the breakdown of the land's natural drainage system ahead of the predicted heavy rains. A sea of mud was the result, which was hardly the ideal ground for an infantry attack. So began the battle that also became known as the Battle of Passchendaele, a small Belgian town a few miles into German held territory.

Because of the rain and the extensive damage to the land, the Flanders lowlands became a virtual swamp in places. These conditions rendered tank mobility ineffective, and at times, all but neutralised infantry movement. With the furious and well prepared German defensive system it was not until August 16th that a major attack was possible. This resulted in small gains for the British at the Battle of Langemark. The picture on page 84 shows British stretcher bearers bringing a wounded man back to a casualty clearing station through the mud of the Ypres salient on August 1st, the day after the advance began! How could they possibly get through in such conditions?

There followed the Battles of the Menin Road Bridge, Polygon Wood and Broodseinde that culminated in the British possession of the ridge east of Ypres. Despite the worsening rain and the weariness of the British troops the High Command decided to carry on the attack, they believed that the Germans were more exhausted!

The Battles of Poelcappelle and Passchendaele on October 9th and 12 were fought by extremely battle-weary attackers. They floundered in the mud against the introduction of German reserves using mustard gas! Finally in late October under political pressure to uphold national pride, British and Canadian forces captured Passchendaele itself. The campaign was finally called-off in November, the clearing of the way to the Belgian coast postponed. The final stages of the Third Battle of Ypres are to be found in later pages.

Photograph by courtesy of the Imperial War Musuem

ATTACK – Siegfried Sassoon. M.C.

At dawn the ridge emerges massed and dun
In wild purple of the glow'ring sun,
Smouldering through spouts of drifting smoke that shroud
The menacing scarred slope; and, one by one,
Tanks creep and topple forward to the wire.
The barrage roars and lifts. Then clumsily bowed
With bombs and guns and shovels and battle gear,
Men jostle and climb to meet the bristling fire.
Lines of grey, muttering faces, masked with fear,
They leave their trenches, going over the top,
While time ticks blank and busy on their wrists,
And hope, with furtive eyes and grappling fists,
Flounders in the mud. O Jesus make it stop!

On August 4th Liberia declared war on Germany. China followed suit on the 14th. On September 29th the British forces in Mesopotamia captured Ramadi . This was a decisive defeat of the Turkish army and was a success for the Anglo-Indian force using motorised transport, armoured cars and cavalry.

On September 26th Brazil declared war on Germany.

6
OCTOBER - DECEMBER 1917
Autumn, Still Awaiting Good News

In the Urban District of Cuckfield there were some 430 houses. Except for perhaps thirty or forty in the "congested business" area of the town they all had good gardens. Despite this there were upwards of 160 allotments cultivating about eleven acres, the greater part of which were growing potatoes. The Urban Council owned 75 allotments and had purchased two spraying machines, which they made available for a nominal charge. The Sergison estate had 50 allotment tenants, and the Burial Board twenty five.

A columnist in the *Mid Sussex Times* described a cutting from a Sussex paper of 1837, and under the heading "Cuckfield Allotments", it stated that an allotment system was about to be introduced in Cuckfield. Mr R Trotter of Borde Hill had acquired three acres of land from Mr Tester of Brook Street. He would let the land to *"worthy and industrious individuals to put into a state of cultivation"*. Mr Trotter's idea was well founded, not to say prophetic.

Mr W Ashdown of Station Road, Burgess Hill, claimed to have cut a marrow in September, 2ft 10ins long and 3ft 1ins in girth weighing 60lbs.

The Chief Constable of East Sussex issued a public notice regarding air raid warnings. Where sirens were not in use, police and special constables would warn the public with three short blasts followed by one long blast, repeated at fifteen second intervals, three times. The all-clear was three short blasts with a fifteen-second interval, confused? The public were advised to stay indoors during an air raid and not collect in crowds outside to watch. Air raids had become a daily occurrence over England.

An anonymous Cuckfield soldier sent an amusing "send-up" from Salonika to the *Mid Sussex Times:*

Beautiful Balkans for the holidays. Bright, briny and breezy.
Attractions - a war held daily. Aeroplanes and artillery exhibitions. No extra charge for night stunts. Shank's pony to all parts. Big game hunting - Bulgars, Turks, snakes, wild dogs, buckshemules, flies, ants, mosquitoes, creepers, crawlers and jumpers of all species. Fishing - all kinds of fever caught daily.
Mail delivered once a month if otherwise not disposed of.
Bathing - mixed - six persons to one bucket.
Miles and miles away from the noise and worries of civilization and from the influence and flirtations of the opposite sex.

Temperature - boiling point guaranteed.
The Hotel Bivvypole is not five minutes from the front.
Menu - biscuits or bread, bully beef or meat and marmalade occasionally.
Cabbages on view only, watered and fed at 6pm.
The public are requested not to take the cabbage patch as a football pitch.
Quinine is served nightly.

A very clever satirical piece, what a shame that the scribe remains unknown. The British sense of humour prevailed again, it was no wonder that the Boys wanted to get back to "Dear Old Sussex by the Sea".

Sad news arrived of Lance Corporal Laurance Upton, of the Machine Gun Corps, London Regiment. He died in action in France, on September 18th, of wounds received that morning. He was the younger son of Mr and Mrs Upton and the second killed, their eldest son Nathan died in 1915. Around the same time Private Arthur Tree, son of George Tree of Highbridge Mill, was reported wounded.

Haywards Heath and surrounding towns and villages came under a different type of pressure in October. Such was the scale of air raids in London at the end of September, that it caused many people to leave the capital for Mid Sussex, to seek accommodation away from the bombing. They were said to be ready to pay well for rooms and put up with any inconvenience. House agents claimed to have never had so many enquiries for dwellings of from £30 to £50 per annum. Those who wished to dispose of houses at a reasonable figure could easily do so.

On October 1st, for one day only, there was a most successful "bring and buy" sale at the Corner House at the junction of High Street and Broad Street. The event entitled "Our Day" was replicated throughout Mid Sussex. It was in aid of the British Red Cross Society. China, books, furniture, old jewellery, secondhand clothing, boots and shoes and fruit and vegetables were among the many items sold, raising the very large sum of £350.

Two more Cuckfield lads came home on leave with tales to tell their friends and families. Private H Gladman, Royal Engineers, was home from France after thirteen months. He had a back wound caused by shrapnel in 1916 and spent three months in hospital. Then he survived being buried alive when a trench mortar shell exploded nearby. Gunner W Knight, RFA, son of Mr and Mrs Knight of Hanlye Cottages perhaps had a pint or two on the following. He had been in France thirteen months, twice wounded, in the left leg and in the back of the neck. When he started his leave, the Germans bombed the railway station in France as he was getting on the train. In the channel his ship encountered a submarine but escaped. At Victoria Station in London he found himself in the middle of an air raid. Whew!!

In the *Mid Sussex Times* of October 9th readers found the following two thought provoking items, first:

Waste not, want not! We are running a race - a strenuous race - a food race with Germany. The one who cannot last the course loses. Staying power is the power. Only one side can win. There's no second prize; no third; no consolation. It's victory, absolute; or defeat, entire. In other words, who starves first comes in last - famished and finished.

The other was an advert from the International Stores, suggesting that there might be a shortage of tea in the next few months. This difficulty could be overcome by drinking coffee for breakfast. The editor of the *National Food Journal*, a Ministry of Food publication, was also asking the public to cooperate in food economy by drinking coffee instead of tea.

The Urban District Council at its October meeting resolved to sell its mangel crop, grown at the Sewage Farm, through T Bannister & Co. in Haywards Heath. It also accepted an offer of £10 for its carrot crop. The council played an important part in horticulture and farming. Its commitment to allotments previously mentioned, it was particularly supportive of the potato market. At the same meeting the council decided to purchase twelve enamel plaques inscribed with the name, "Fireman". These were for fixing to the doors of the town's firefighters. At this meeting the Surveyor, also the Head Fireman, reported a successful trial of a new system for improving the time for arriving at an emergency. Boy Scouts were used as runners, knocking-up the firemen, it only taking twenty minutes for all personnel to arrive on the scene. It was said however, that the amount of available hose connected to a fire hydrant was not sufficient to reach some of the houses.

The majority of Cuckfield families had one or more relatives in the forces. With each month the death toll continued to rise. The daily anxiety of waiting for news must have been unbelievable, and that waiting must have become part of everyday life. In a small community, knowledge of one family's grief was soon known to all. And so it went on

Private James Rowland, Royal Sussex Regiment died in action on September 26th. He joined-up at the start of the war, severely wounded twice, only to be declared fit to fight again. In the letter to his parents he was yet another who had died soon after being hit, and didn't *"suffer very much"*.

On October 4th, also killed in action, was Lance Corporal Percy Selby, Royal Warwickshire Regiment. Just twenty years of age he had been a cowman at Sidnye Farm. Percy joined-up at the outbreak of the war, wounded in 1916, and after spending some months in hospital in England returned to France in January 1917. He was the fourth son of Mr and Mrs Selby of Brook Street and the second to be lost in the war. William was killed in 1914.

Mr and Mrs Anscombe of Albany Villas, Broad Street, learned of the death of their son Private F Anscombe, Royal Warwickshire Regiment, killed in action on October 7th. Like the other two, he joined-up at the beginning. He was wounded in 1916 and spent some time in hospital, returning to the front in July 1917. He played an active part in the Empire Day celebrations at the school in April (see page 48). With the news of his death came the expected letter from his commanding officer:

> Please accept . . . The Huns had put up a strong counter attack one morning, and the front line Battalion had practically used up all its ammunition, so I was called to take a party of 100 men up with a further supply. The journey was a terrible one, but the men were heroes every one. Your son's death was, from a soldier's point of view, a glorious one. He gave his all to try to help his comrades in distress. God will reward him . . .

There is something depressingly familiar about these last three losses. All went off to fight at the outbreak of hostilities, all wounded and all mended to fight again. It must be really hoped, that the loved ones of all those killed waiting in places like Cuckfield, gained comfort from the letters they received.

As well as those killed others were wounded. Lieutenant Stanley Wood, the third son of Mrs James Wood of Sunny Bank, Broad Street, was severely wounded and was in hospital in Rouen. Mrs Wood's fourth son (page 72), was still in hospital and progressing favourably. Then came the news that Lance Corporal J M Ansell, Royal Engineers was posted missing. He had only recently rejoined his unit after a shrapnel wound in the face.

AUTUMN - Siegfried Sassoon M.C.

October's bellowing anger breaks and cleaves
The bronzed battalions of the stricken wood
In whose lament I hear a voice that grieves
For battle's fruitless harvest, and the feud
Of outraged men. Their lives are like the leaves
Scattered in flocks of ruin, tossed and blown
Along the westering furnace flaring red.
O martyred youth and manhood overthrown,
The burden of your wrongs is on my head.

The less well-off of Cuckfield were pleased to learn that the Urban District Council had secured a limited quantity of coal for sale to cottagers in the forthcoming winter. This action also covered Ansty, Brook Street and Slough Green. The matter had become particularly important, due the shortage of coal in East Sussex, with the problem being most acute in the Eastbourne area. The Council placed an advert in the local paper offering coal to cottagers. (Tradesmen, shop-owners etc. did not qualify). Price per cwt was 1s 10d, and was to be collected from the Council's yard in London Lane. Prior application had to be made to Mr S Knight, at Brocketts in Whiteman's Green, before November 10th.

On October 23rd there was a report of a fire at Copyhold Cottage. Among those in the house were the Hon. Mrs Lyon and Mrs Dalton. The building was burnt to the ground, despite the telephoned alarm call. This highlighted the inadequacies of the alarm system and the need for a more efficient arrangement. At that time, the Police Superintendent at Haywards Heath was responsible for alerting the Fire Brigade. Due to a staff problem he had to go to the Captain of the local Fire Brigade to inform him of the emergency. Of course the press took up the story and urged the authorities in Cuckfield and Haywards Heath to provide telephones for their fire fighters. The total loss of Copyhold Cottage that highlighted inefficiencies, totalled between £2,000 and £3,000, fortunately covered by insurance.

> Tom Wells tells the story that, according to his father, rumour had it that Bert Croucher, Cuckfield's Surveyor and Head Fireman, cycled from Glebe Road to Copyhold Cottage to measure up to determine how much hose would be needed. Taking no chances!

There had been some humorous remarks made in the press regarding Cuckfield's firefighting ability, but this incident must have provoked a serious outcome.

People were desperate for entertainment. The Picture Theatre in Haywards Heath was extremely popular and it was only a "short walk" from Cuckfield. The more wealthy residents could easily travel to Brighton where there were several theatres and cinemas, but the eagerly anticipated local concerts were available to the majority.

On October 22nd a prestigious concert took place in the old Drill Hall. There were two performances, the first, with dearer seats in the afternoon and the second, with less expensive ones in the evening. It was described as a musical treat. Organised by Mrs Preston of Cuckfield Park and Mrs Lampson of Moonhill Place, it was in aid of the Cuckfield VAD Hospital and the District Nursing Association. People came from Burgess Hill, Lindfield and Haywards Heath as well as Cuckfield, together with many of the hospital patients.

Mrs Preston sang *"Starry Woods"* and *"Bird of Love Devine"* as solos and a duet with Mr W Pitt Chapman, *"The Sweetest Flower that Blows"*. Mrs Lampson played a piano solo, Liszt's *"Study in D Flat"* and then formed part of a trio with Mrs Robertson and Miss Parker, violin and cello. They all played solos to great applause. The concert's climax was a humorous one, with Dr Houston Collison presenting a sketch called *"A Parochial Concert"*. Both performances were immensely successful and a tribute to all those concerned. The press reported it as a huge success raising £40 towards the two good causes.

Two ladies received an accolade. Mrs Bannister, the matron of Cuckfield's VAD Hospital, received official recognition for her administration work. Miss Bevan's nursing abilities at the hospital were honoured. Their names placed before the Secretary for War for the valuable services rendered in connection with war nursing.

Mr Sharman of Lindfield grew a pumpkin weighing 88 lbs. He arranged a "guess the number of seeds" competition, the winner receiving four shillings. He then sold the seeds at two for a penny. All the proceeds in aid of the local Auxiliary Hospital.

One Sussex Tribunal excused a man from military service on the grounds that he was the father of nine children. He was told to go home to his family. Whether this was a reward or punishment was not made clear.

The Urban District Council at their November meeting had before them a letter from "The Comrades of the Great War", and resolved to support them. Organisations were being formed to help those soldiers, sailors and airmen wounded and were on hard times. The council received the Surveyor's report regarding the state of the elm trees at Whiteman's Green. It was resolved that they should be topped and the dead ones replaced by limes. The saga of Cuckfield's fire fighting ability was furthered. The council resolved to place a list of names and addresses of its firemen at the Queen's Hall, Whiteman's Green and Broad Street. They were D Carter, South Street; S Wilsman, Ockenden Lane; J Carter, Mytten Cottage; W Reeves, London Lane; A Line, The Gasworks; J Webb, Ruthven Stables and A Mays, Broad Street.

Communal Kitchens were being introduced as a means of aiding the poor and to help with hot meals for schoolchildren. Lewes' kitchen had been operating for about five months and was serving on average 500 portions per day. East Grinstead's was in full swing and Haywards Heath's was in the throes of starting. Cuckfield started a hot meal's service at the school which was attended by about 120 each day. A typical meal was three-quarters of a pint of good nourishing stew, occasionally with dumplings, and two ounces of bread.

For the month of November, Cuckfield's Food Control Committee, announced the maximum price for butter as 2s 4d per lb and the retail price of milk at 6d per quart.

The war was making little progress in terms of finishing. Stalemate was still on most people's minds. With the towns and villages denuded of their young (and in some cases not so young) came more disturbing news. The *Mid Sussex Times* leader writer warned of a rumour that the Army authorities were looking for yet more men *"to lay aside their civilian attire for khaki"*. He even suggested that under the system of medical examination about to be reviewed, many men passed fit, never were, and had become burdens on the country. However, men dissatisfied that their medical grade kept them from fighting, were urged to re-apply under a new system of examination. Whether this latest trawl for more men to fill the trenches was successful is debatable. (In May 1918 the Government raised the age of conscription to 51).

By the end of November Cuckfield's Food Control Committee had raised the price of butter to 2s 6d per lb. The Gas Company increased the price of gas to 5s per therm.

On November 25th a Thanksgiving Service was held to mark the Army's victory at Cambrai. Good news, hard to come by, was celebrated at the Holy Trinity.

The Cuckfield Women's Suffrage Society was busy in December. On Saturday 1st, they arranged a well attended Jumble Sale at the Congregational Church Schoolroom in aid of Scottish Women's Hospitals. Women present included Miss E Payne, Miss A Payne, Miss Chute Ellis, Miss Armitage, Miss Turner, Miss Bristow, Miss Gill, Mrs Fuller and Mrs Cheale. Most of these appeared in *Kelly's* Directory under the heading of "Private Residents" of Cuckfield. The Suffrage movement was particularly strong at the Congregational Church. The Payne family had been senior members at that church for many years. Also, sponsored by the Society was a lantern lecture held at the church schoolroom. The lecturer was a Miss Holmes and the subject, her experiences in Romania and Russia during the war. She was with the Motor Transport Section of the Scottish Women's Hospitals (London Unit). Chairman for the afternoon was the Reverend S Maddock who pronounced the lecture informative and successful. A collection made was given to the Scottish Women's Hospital, which, with the proceeds from the Jumble Sale amounted to over £25.

The most recently formed Women's Institute was at Balcombe. Cuckfield had not yet joined with Wivelsfield (the first), Scaynes Hill, Lindfield and Burgess Hill in forming a W I. It was very much the trend to band women together, to meet each month and discuss matters of interest in the home. Discussions held exchanging ideas on food economy, recipes, clothes etc., and how to improve their war effort. A prime objective was to integrate all sections of town and village life. However, at this, Balcombe's second meeting a lady speaker from Cuckfield was to have given a talk on Cuckfield's war savings achievements. She was unfortunately unable to be present, but the Balcombe Secretary deputised. Cuckfield's War Savings Association was the subject. Balcombe's members were impressed to learn that after a slightly difficult start in January 1917, Cuckfield's savers had raised, often in sixpences, £907 to date. They were urged to follow their neighbour's example and save for the country.

At the December meeting of the Cuckfield Urban District Council it was resolved to invest a further £300 in the 5% War Loan. On December 11th came an appeal from the Council on behalf of the Government for scrap metal and other inorganic waste. It was stated that these were necessary for *"Munitions and other purposes connected with the prosecution of the War".*

Times were indeed hard or heartless, the Board of Guardians decided unanimously, following Miss E Payne's proposition, that the Poor Law Institution's inmates would receive no extras at Christmas. The members of the board quibbled over the question of Christmas extras; debating whether to give the inmates Christmas puddings without butter, perhaps substituting carrots, raisins and currants were hard to get etc., etc. Then came Miss Payne's resolution citing the Food Controller's orders, the debate ended abruptly. All that happened at the November meeting. In December 11th's issue of the *Mid Sussex Times* there was "The Christmas Appeal for the Workhouse Inmates". Mr E J Waugh the Clerk to the Guardians, made an appeal to the people residing in the area of the Cuckfield Union. He asked them to send some toys for the children, and apples for the inmates. Some gifts of money but no apples had been received. The newspaper article went on to point out that the children and old folk in the House would not be having their usual Christmas treat provided by the Guardians. This, being due to The Ministry of Food's regulations. It finishes by asking for money and promising to publish the names of donors in the next edition. Mr Waugh said that if each inmate received a new sixpence it would create a little joy in the hearts of all.

No further news on the subject was reported. The week after the appeal, a note in "Wideawake's" column in the *Mid Sussex Times* said:

> A tradesman sends me the following :- "Re your recent remarks about tea. I saw in a railway van in Cuckfield a few days since a box containing 40 lbs of tea for a household of five people, and I, a grocer with upwards of 1,000 customers to supply, could not get a pound for three weeks. Is this justice?" No, it's a ——— shame.

The Board of Guardians at their December meeting decided to re-invest £25 in a War Loan. At the same meeting they discussed the lack of apples. Nothing more on the inmates Christmas.

The bells of the Parish Church peeled on December 11th to celebrate the capture of Jerusalem.

As mentioned earlier, every fortnight a thank-you note appeared in the *Mid Sussex Times* from the patients and staff of Cuckfield's VAD Hospital, for the various gifts, received. The giving of vegetables, fruit and other foodstuffs had become a regular feature of Cuckfield's support for its hospital. The final thank-you for 1917 came on Christmas Day. The list of contributors included, Miss Bevan, Mrs Brougham, Mrs S Clarke, Mrs Denny, Miss Huckett, Mrs Huth, Mrs Bannister, Mrs Reid, Mrs Schlesinger, Mrs R Cooper, Mrs Wells, Lady Kleinwort, Mrs Rate and Mr Caffyn.

The year was drawing to a close, and the effort required from the majority of the civilian population had become increasingly severe. Britain was a country generally opposed to the idea of food rationing, but it was coming. During the year the imposition of controls had increased. With so many men away, Christmas would be bad enough, but the cry for more frugality was much in evidence. From the *Mid Sussex Times* on December 25th, yes the paper was published on Christmas Day, was the observation:

> The working classes of this country do not object so much to food shortage as to the knowledge that some people can obtain plenty whilst others are short! They protest not against shortage but against the inequality that exists today. There are

undoubtedly, thousands of well-to-do people who are acting on the square and are very frugal in the use of all kinds of foodstuffs. All honour to them! They are true patriots. And we know they will not chide us for going for those who are "not playing the game". . . they are their country's enemies. If ever compulsory rationing is forced it will be the food hogs who will be the cause of it. We want voluntary rationing to continue if possible. We have heard of the evils of compulsory rationing at different meetings, but one cannot fail to recognise that for that system there is something to be said.

A letter from the Chief Constable of Staffordshire in *The Times*, commenting on food queues said:

No possible process of distribution to retailers can be of any real use unless each person is restricted to his fair and proper share; rationing there must be, and the sooner the better; otherwise greedy selfish people, with more time and money to spare, will continue to obtain more than their share of the national supply of food necessaries, and others will have to go without. The silly farce of putting self indulgent people "on their honour" not to eat is played out.

Lord Rhondda, the Food Controller at the Ministry of Food decided that there would be one meatless day per week after January 1st. Cooked and uncooked meats would not be sold on that day. Also, it was proposed that meat sold by butchers after that date, would be reduced by 25% from the amount sold by them in the October quarter.

As the year ended more news came of some of Cuckfield's servicemen. Private Joseph Markwick, wounded on December 8th, died the same day. On August 8th he was wounded, recovered, and then returned to fight. Captain R S Clarke of Borde Hill had been wounded. He was progressing satisfactorily, *"the bullet having been extracted and the lung healing"*. On a happier note Sergeant Armitage married Miss Dorothy Chadwick of Forest Row. Mr and Mrs John Bennett of 1 Fern Cottages, Brainsmeade, had just heard of their son's promotion to Sergeant in the Machine Gun Corps. Lance Corporal Harry Murrell, Royal Fusiliers, whose parents lived in Brook Street, was commended for distinguished bravery in the field on December 6th. The Military Cross was awarded to Captain Montague Turner, Royal Sussex Regiment.

The Cuckfield Club decided to cancel its Christmas social re-union. So many of its members were either away fighting or were no longer around. There was also the belief that many members who were available would not wish to attend.

The vicar made it known through the *Parish Magazine*, that a plea had come from the Ministry of Labour, urging more women to come forward to take up manual work. He felt the women of Cuckfield were really doing their utmost anyway. But, if any person wished to know more, he was to be contacted.

The townspeople of Cuckfield prepared themselves for the fourth Christmas of the war. The churches were full, there was no overt jingoism, only prayer for a speedy end to the war and the safe return of loved ones.

Christmas celebrations in Cuckfield included an organ recital by Mr Fred Knight, the music teacher, at the Congregational Church. He also played the violin. The whole evening was a well-arranged music concert with other soloists, Miss Winifred Cleare, violin, and Miss Edith Bristow the piano. Violin duets were played between Mr Knight and Miss Cleare. The full audience enjoyed the music of Bach, Mendelssohn and Gounot among others.

The Parish Church's announcement about Christmas services stressed, that it could not be for any, a time of merriment. It was to be hoped that some quiet joy of Christmas could come into many homes, even where there was sorrow of bereavement and the anxiety of separation.

As an octogenarian retired farmer rather wisely concluded, he could never remember such a quiet Christmas time. Never, was a Christmas so unlike Christmas, apart from the weather. It snowed very heavily the previous week.

This final period of 1917 at home was very depressing, how were things progressing over there? What were the Servicemen's thoughts at the end of 1917?

DREAMERS - Siefried Sassoon M.C.

Soldiers are citizens of death's grey land,
  Drawing no dividend from time's to-morrows.
In the great hour of destiny they stand,
  Each with his feuds, and jealousies, and sorrows.
Soldiers are sworn to action; they must win
  Some flaming, fatal climax with their lives.
Soldiers are dreamers; when the guns begin
  They think of firelit homes, clean beds and wives.

I see them in foul dug-outs, gnawed by rats,
  And in the ruined trenches, lashed with rain,
Dreaming of things they did with balls and bats,
  And mocked by hopeless longing to regain
Bank-holidays, and picture shows, and spats,
  And going to the office in the train.

FATIGUE

In this final summary of the war so far we will see the Allied offensive operations on the Western Front fade out with the onset of winter. At the end of 1917 the winter stalemate arrived. Tired armies faced each other on the Western Front and in the east the Russian effort had collapsed following the October Revolution.

In October in Flanders, the Third Battle of Ypres was still being fought. As we have learned the final action at Passchendaele took place on the 12th. The village itself was taken on November 6th. By this time it had become obvious that the winter and the defender had triumphed again. The main offensive was called off, but localised fighting, as always, continued. The picture shows troops of the Canadian 4th Division holding the line at Passchendaele. A machine gun position in the mud! November 14th.

It is not the purpose of this book to record the minute detail of any of the battles, large or small. There are many full histories of all the campaigns. The success or failure of the war was measured by the results of the major offensives. The Third Battle of Ypres was one of these and turned out to be another of the failures. The name Passchendaele would be coupled with the Somme as synonymous with military carnage. For the gaining of five miles (lost in a matter of months) the British Army lost 300,000 casualties and the estimated German losses, 200,000. The scale of individual bravery was monumental and there were many medals awarded to men from Mid Sussex.

Photograph by courtesy of the Imperial War Museum.

> The whole campaign was fought in an area of land not much bigger than Mid Sussex. Territory gained was not much more than the distance from Cuckfield to Burgess Hill. The British preliminary bombardment of 3,000 guns fired over four million shells in the ten days before the attack. Half a million men were killed or wounded. A significant action was the attack and capture of a small wood, Polygon Wood. It is difficult to realise a situation where hundreds and hundreds of men would be fighting over say, New England Wood.

The final German - Russian engagement of the war was at the Battle of

Riga, a strategic Baltic port (now the capital of Latvia). Launched on September 1st, the battle was a complete success for Germany, driving the Russians from the Gulf of Riga by October 11th.

On October 24th a German army joined the Austrians in an attack on Caporetto in Northern Italy. A theatre of war less active than the Western Front now became important as the successful Austro-German offensive pushed many miles into Italy. They were finally stopped fifty kilometres north of Venice. The Italians and the Austro-Hungarian armies had been fighting in the Alps since declaring war in May 1915. First one side and then the other would launch an attack. The Italians had just completed the eleventh Isonzo offensive. German intervention strengthened the Austrian effort, resulting in French and British troops being despatched to the Italian Front for the first time, stabilizing it by December 30th.

The Palestine campaign really deserves more space than is available here. In previous chapters there had been news of Cuckfield men there. The strategic value of the Suez canal was the motivation for the British, Australian, New Zealand and Indian troops fighting Turkey for control of the region. Palestine had been part of the Ottoman Empire for four centuries. Following the arrival of modern aircraft, Bristol Fighters, the Royal Flying Corps regained control of the air. On October 31st the British captured the Beersheba-Gaza Line. The initiative now lay firmly in the hands of the British and the advance into Palestine represented the best prospects for an Allied success in 1918. The army commanded by General Allenby captured Jerusalem on December 9th, a victory greatly heralded in Britain, bringing much needed good news, relieving the gloom of France and Flanders.

By early November the Revolution in Russia rendered that country no longer able or willing to play a part in the war. The same day saw British forces in Mesopotamia capture Tikrit, the campaign was going well. Unfortunately, the successful Army Commander General Maude died of cholera on November 18th.

On November 20th the final Allied attack on the Western Front began. This was the Battle of Cambrai in Artois, southeast of Arras, directed against the famous German Hindenberg Line defences. It was a historic battle, the first in which tanks were used in large numbers, and in a truly attacking role. The British Third Army commanded by General Byng, whose Canadian forces had captured Vimy Ridge in April during the Arras campaign, gave approval for the tank attack. At first Field Marshal Haig vetoed the plan. When it was apparent, that the Ypres campaign would fail, he was persuaded to seek a victory in another location as a morale booster before the year end. Byng planned a breakthrough, despite the lack of adequate reserves and the seemingly perpetual vagaries of the weather. Six infantry and two cavalry divisions with 476 Mark IV tanks launched the attack along a six-mile front.

> A MILE OF FRONT. When we read about a front of so many miles, it is worth considering what this means in materiel. What is required to fortify one mile of front? There would be first and second lines of trenches with the communication trenches and breastworks. The necessary barbed wire for these would amount to 900 miles, weighing 110 tons. The sandbags required for protecting them numbered six and a quarter millions. That number if laid end to end would stretch across Europe, from North Cape in Norway, to the southern most point in Greece. To fill these millions of sandbags, and place them in position, would keep 500 men hard at work for twelve months. In addition to this amount of wire and sandbags, wooden posts would be required, 12,000 six-foot standards, 12,000 small pickets, more than a million feet of timber as well as 35,000 feet of corrugated iron and vast quantities of rivetting material of various kinds. It is virtually impossible to comprehend the enormity of it all. These statistics were found in the *Mid Sussex Times* of October 30th 1917.

The initial success was good, gaining a depth of four miles in some sectors. Sadly, the tank was not wholly reliable, its mechanical breakdown responsible for many losses. Others suffered direct hits from enemy artillery. The village of Flesquieres was taken but the lack of reserves coupled with the arrival of substantial German reinforcements blocked the way to Cambrai. On November 30th, twenty divisions of German troops launched a counter attack, recovering the ground lost to the opening British drive.

Photography by courtesy of the Imperial War Museum

However the British public was only too pleased to learn of the triumph of the tanks and herald it as a victory at Cambrai. Actually the real success was the fact that the tank's potential was proven. The beginning of mobile warfare had arrived, although there was still much to do on the tank's design. The Battle of Cambrai at the time was regarded as a failure to exploit a rare opportunity. As usual the casualty rate was very high, in less than two weeks 45,000 British and 50,000 Germans were added to the ever increasing list.

The year ended with significant British progress in Egypt and Mesopotamia. Salonika was static, a new commander, General Marie Guillaumat was appointed in December to "make things happen". The Germans had lost their African colonies. The submarine war was still threatening Britain's food supply. The Western Front was no nearer under control for the Russian end had passed the initiative back to the Germans. The huge build-up of American troops in France was giving the French renewed hope. On December 31st United States warships joined the British Grand fleet.

ANTHEM FOR DOOMED YOUTH - Wilfred Owen M.C.

What passing-bells for these who die as cattle?
- Only the montrous anger of the guns.
Only the stuttering rifles' rapid rattle
Can patter out their hasty orisons.
No mockeries now for them; no prayers or bells;
Nor any voice of mourning save the choirs, -
The shrill, demented choirs of wailing shells;
And bugles calling for them from sad shires.

What candles may be held to speed them all?
Not in hands of boys but in their eyes
Shall shine the holy glimmers of goodbyes.
The pallor of girls' brows shall be their pall;
Their flowers the tenderness of patient minds,
And each slow dusk a drawing-down of blinds.

THE ROYAL SUSSEX REGIMENT

35TH FOOT

107TH FOOT

It is appropriate to include a little about the Royal Sussex Regiment. Rather more than half of those who left Cuckfield to join the armed services in the Great War, served with the County Regiment. The following, is a but a brief insight into the Regiment's history, with particular regard to 1917. The Regiment was formed in 1701 and during the 18th Century fought with great distinction at the famous Battles of Quebec and Bunker Hill. Prominent parts were played in the capture of Malta, at the beginning of the 19th Century, in Italy and in India, during the Mutiny of 1857. The South African War at the turn of the Century saw the Regiment in full action. On August 4th 1914 it consisted of six battalions, two regular, the 1st and 2nd, one militia and three Territorials. By October 1915 a number of additional battalions were raised. By 1917, twenty-three Battalions of the Royal Sussex Regiment took their place in the British Army. They served in all the theatres of the war and at home. This meant that in the order of 30,000 men were in, or joined the Regiment, between 1914 and 1918, of which 6,800 lost their lives.

The 1st Battalion was in India at the outbreak of war. It remained there to serve on the North-West Frontier as the only regular British troops retained in India.

The 2nd Battalion landed in France on August 13th 1914, joining the BEF's 2nd Brigade, 1st Division. The Battalion held in reserve for the Battle of Mons, had its first action in the Battle of the Marne in September 1914 (Page 8). It remained in constant combat throughout 1914, including playing a significant part in the First Battle of Ypres. Here it earned the name "The Iron Regiment", conferred upon it by German prisoners captured on November 1st. In those two months the 2nd Battalion lost 800 casualties. These were made up by replacements which included men from Cuckfield, sadly some died.

Available records show that Cuckfield's soldiers joined the 4th, 7th, 8th, 9th, 11th and 13th Battalions. Some probably transferred to other regiments as the war progressed. The 4th Battalion served in Gallipoli and Egypt, including the Jerusalem campaign, from August 1915 until May 1918, when it joined the BEF in France. The other battalions all took part in the France and Flanders campaigns. All fought at the Battle of the Somme in July 1916.

In 1917, the 2nd Battalion was at the Battle of Messines and the Third Battle of Ypres, Passchendale, with a great number of casualties. The 7th

Battalion fought at Arras in April, local fighting during May to July, and then after intensive training with tanks, the Battle of Cambrai in November.

The 8th Battalion was a Pioneer Battalion serving with distinction in the BEF's 18th Division. Its work comprised the laying of tracks, the construction of light railways, building shelters, digging trenches and most times under heavy enemy fire. The 9th Battalion fought at Arras, Vimy Ridge, Messines and Third Ypres.

The 11th, 12th and 13th (Southdown) Battalions arrived in France in March 1916. Following the Somme campaign all three were stationed at Ypres from December 1916, where they remained in and out of the trenches, until January 1918. This was a very long tour of duty in such a strenuous sector of the war. They were heavily involved in the Third Battle of Ypres from August 1917, fighting at Menin Road, Polygon Wood and Passchendaele.

In February 1918 the 12th Battalion was disbanded, its troops being sent to other battalions of the Regiment. The 11th and 13th Battalions took part in some very fierce fighting during the German Offensive of March 1918. Both battalions were practically wiped out. In April 1918 the 13th Battalion was all but destroyed at Kemmel. The survivors were absorbed into other units, the 13th as a battalion played no further part in the war.

A well-known myth of the war was that soldiers spent most of their time in the trenches. This was not a fact however, the British system based on a monthly rotation, was devised to allow an infantryman to spend one week in the front lines. This week was split between the fire trench and the support trench. One week was spent in reserve and the remaining period behind the line.

It is recorded nonetheless, that the 11th Battalion of the Royal Sussex Regiment spent thirty-five continuous days in the trenches without relief during the Somme campaign.

Boredom was a constant companion in the trenches. The picture shows a typical time of inactivity, possibly a lull in fighting, or maybe a spell in the reserve trench. Although not the Royal Sussex Regiment, they must have shared similar experiences. Note the soldier writing, probably a letter home. His comrades can be seen catching up on lost sleep despite the horrible looking conditions.

Photograph courtesy of the Imperial War Museum, London

The Regiment was to cease as an entity, in itself, in 1966. Fortunately its memory lives on with its thriving Regimental Association, its excellent museum in Eastbourne and its extensive archive collection at County Records in Chichester. The Royal Sussex Regiment's successor today is The Princess of Wales' Royal Regiment.

Badge and Colours of the First Battalion The Royal Sussex Regiment

Epilogue

Thus, did the year of 1917 end. It was to be nearly another year before the war finished with the Armistice on November 11th 1918.

The short reviews of the war as described in this narrative have been but a brief glimpse of the whole story. Sufficient, it is hoped, for those not familiar with the history of the Great War to improve their understanding. For the expert, the reviews are perhaps just potted versions of a layman's research. The idea is to try to empathise with our forebears all those years ago. The stories of the people, and events at home have been gleaned from newspapers, the Church Magazines, County Records, as well as first hand recollections and many other sources.

What of the war to the end of 1917? Away from the Western Front the British were successfully pursuing their aims, apart from the disaster at Gallipoli. In France and Flanders as we have seen the large scale offensives had failed. There had been victories on both sides, the Allies in their major drives and the Germans with counter attacks. Localised fighting, attacks on towns, villages, woods, road systems etc. happened throughout the year. The trench line of defence remained unconquerable. It was the relatively small areas of land over which the battles took place, and such vast armies met, that is so mind numbing. But to win the war either a major offensive had to really succeed, or one side had to be battered into defeat.

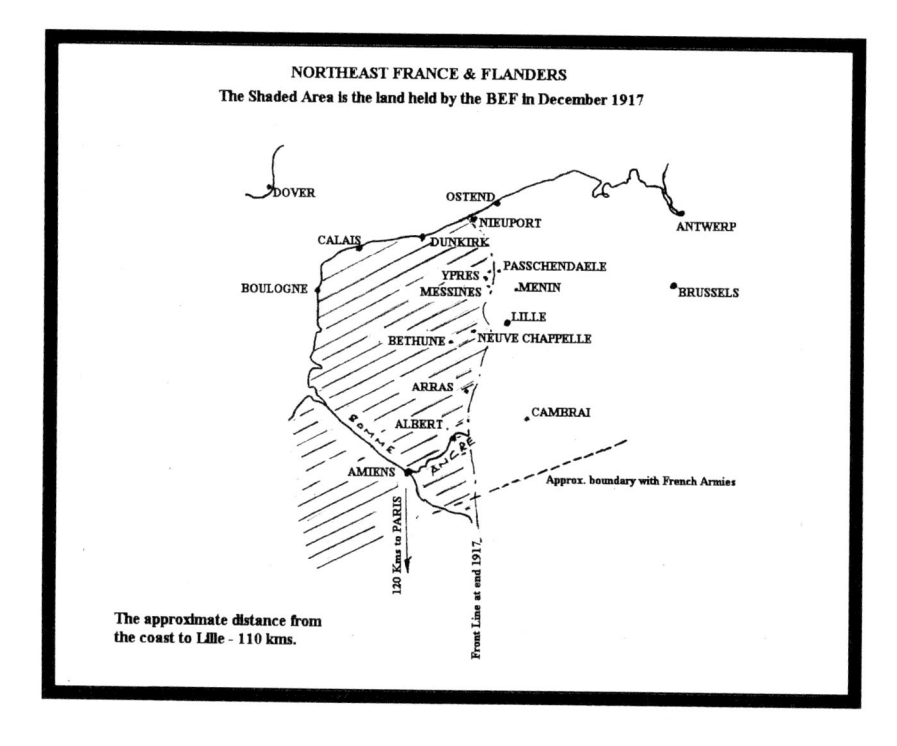

NORTHEAST FRANCE & FLANDERS
The Shaded Area is the land held by the BEF in December 1917

The approximate distance from the coast to Lille - 110 kms.

Trenches had been dug by both sides, stretching from Nieuport to the Swiss border. British interest however, was always concentrated in the northeast corner of France and part of Belgian Flanders. The map shows that very small area of land occupied by the BEF for much of the war. Compare the distances, the coast to Lille, only 110 kms and Amiens to Paris 120 kms. As we have seen, the huge offensives of the Somme and Passchendaele took place in such small parts of the countryside. It was as if the participants were reliving medieval battle strategy, or at best Napoleonic times when the combatants met in a field to determine the outcome. This time there was the added complication of modern weaponry, artillery, machine guns and barbed wire, not to mention poison gas.

The means were in the future of moving an army about quickly and efficiently. As were the fast armoured division, lorried infantry and a truly effective air force. The Politicians and the Generals on both sides learnt very quickly that when the Germans dug the first trenches, stopping the war was the sensible option. But, there was no mechanism for a political solution. Perhaps that is another story.

Wilfred Owen wrote in January 1917, *"It is pock-marked like the body of foulest disease, and its odour is the breath of cancer . . . No Man's Land under snow is like the face of the moon, chaotic, crater ridden, uninhabitable, awful, the abode of madness."*

At home, 1917 was to be the year when the civilian would become totally enmeshed in the conflict. It was a year for confronting food problems. War savings schemes were rigorously pursued. The National Service movement was created seeking volunteers, men and women, to leave home for munitions work and agriculture.

Cuckfield's hospital was busier than before, treating between 300 and 400 patients in 1917. The report of the VAD Hospital for 1917 was fulsome in its praise for the many gifts, the money received, helping to alleviate the hardships of the wounded men. Other praiseworthy matters included, the help given by *"12 to 15 of our poorer neighbours"*. They took in laundry work for two or three patients each, some since the beginning of the war. It sounds condescending today to refer to our poorer neighbours but, in 1917 it seemed quite acceptable. Mrs B Y Bevan was thanked for providing accommodation for the night nurse, at no charge for a period, of three months. Then there were those who met regularly at the hospital to mend badly worn clothes, linen etc. There was thanks also for those who took mending home. The Hospital closed on December 31st 1918.

The War Hospital Supply Depot at Cuckfield Park opened in 1915, called upon the women to make many items required by hospitals, such as bandages, sunshields, pyjamas etc. By December 1918, 38,338 different articles had been supplied. There is plenty of evidence that Cuckfield's women worked hard and by that helped their men away fighting. Amongst those who left home was Alice Godsmark (Connie Salter's mother), she joined the Women's Auxiliary Army Corps, and served in France. Alice M Mitchell, daughter of Mr Mitchell of Percy Cottages was mentioned in despatches. This, was for her work, as a Charge Sister, in the Duchess of Westminster Hospital in Northern France, where she had been for three years.

In fact, in the whole story there are few signs of many lighthearted moments. The main relief came from visits to the cinema in Haywards Heath, the concerts organised in the town on behalf of the war effort and presumably private family moments. The younger children growing up during the war would not have behaved much differently from normal, as remembered in the schoolgirls' "Reminiscences". (It was the same in 1939-45). The church had an immense influence on the daily life of the town as we have seen. Memorial and Thanksgiving services were plentiful. Parishioners relied heavily on the vicar, Canon Wilson, for solace in times of grief, and for his morale boosting sermons for strength to continue. As explained a church service in a rural community was sometimes the prime source of information.

The Women's Institute(WI) organisation was founded in 1897 at Stoney Creek, Ontario, Canada, to nurture the development of community welfare and the practice of rural crafts. The National Federation of Women's Institutes in the UK, with branches in many towns and villages, was founded 1915. The first branch in Mid Sussex was at Wivelsfield and started in 1916. Cuckfield's branch started in 1919. The National Union of Townswomen's Guilds, founded in 1929, is the urban equivalent.

The saga of Cuckfield's firefighting ability continued. On March 3rd, 1918 at 7.15pm a fire broke out in the South Street Laundry. With the aid of the Boy Scout runners, the whole team arrived on site, complete with hose in ten minutes. The fire was however, controlled by a "Mimimax" fire extinguisher. Eventually the town got its fire engine.

Women's suffrage, strong in Cuckfield with evidence pointing to its strength in the Congregational Church, was close. Women's efforts during the war would soon be recognised as promised, in 1918.

We have seen how the school children became involved. They took part in special ceremonies at the school, with particular emphasis on patriotism. Many of them attended church every Sunday, they participated in the Memorial Services and other events that commemorated the war. The children "dug for victory" in the school allotments. For the younger ones there was even a Baby Show.

News eagerly awaited by wives, sweethearts, parents and families came only sparsely and all too often it was bad. On average nearly two deaths were reported each month and probably as many wounded. As we have seen, many of those killed were among the wounded, healed and sent off to fight again until that fateful day.

At the beginning of 1918 the BEF was tired after the unsuccessful offensives of the previous year. The German High Command reasoned that the only way to gain anything from the war, before the American influence had an effect, was to neutralise the BEF quickly. The reinforcing of the German

Western Front armies happened with the arrival of men released from the Russian Front. Their forces increased by 30% from November 1917 to March 1918, whereas British and French manpower had diminished by a quarter.

In other theatres of war the Allied cause met with more rewards. The Middle East and the Balkans were under control. But, as ever, the Western Front was all important and 1918 was the year of resolution. The beginning of the end started in March. The German Spring Offensive (the Kaiserschlact Offensive) began on March 21st, with the aim of splitting the French and British Armies at the Somme. The battles raged from Arras in the north to La Fere, about 90 kilometres south. Although outnumbered by 63 divisions to 26, after retreating many miles, the Allies held the German Army on April 4th just short of Amiens, Kaiserschlact stalled.

On April 9th the Germans launched the Lys Offensive in Flanders. It was an attempt to reach the coast, and on May 27th they started the Third Battle of the Aisne. This latter was their last major effort to end the war before the Americans were ready. The Germans battered their way to the River Marne, within 90 kilometres of Paris by June 3rd. They were close to complete victory, but exhaustion and Allied counter attacks stabilised the situation. Casualties on both sides in all three campaigns were extremely high.

Thus it was in June that the German attacks finally came to a halt. The Americans first campaign in May accelerated through June, culminating in the full Allied offensive that led to the war's end. The British finally broke through the Hindenberg Line in September.

British casualties on the Western Front in 1918 were approximately 850,000, nearly one third of the total for the whole war in France and Flanders.

The town of Cuckfield celebrated the peace. The returning servicemen were joyously welcomed. Events were staged in their honour, including a dinner and of course church services. It was not long before the first meeting was held to discuss a war memorial to honour those who did not return. The peacetime recovery began, but, that **is** another story.

Have you forgotten yet?
Look up, and swear by the green of the spring
that you'll never forget.

from *Aftermath* by **Siegfried Sassoon.**

INDEX

Aisne River	10,58
Allenby General	96
America, AEF, USA etc.	45,58,98
Ancre, Battle of	29
Anglo-Indian Troops	12,43,84,96
Anscombe Reuben	24,38,47,49,52
Anscombe Sgt M	40
Anscombe Pte F	48,87
Ansell L/Cpl J M	53,88
Ansty	21,72
Apps F	48
Archdeaconry of Lewes	21
Armitage Miss	91
Arras, Battle of	42,58,83,96,100
Artois	13,42,58,83,96
Ashdown W	85
Askew Pte L	56
Asqith Mr	14,19
Attewell T	28,47
Attree J	80
Attwater Sgt E	33
Australian/New Zealand Forces	12,96
Austria/Hungary, Army etc	9,12,82,96
Balcombe	22,91
Balkans	18,
Bannister Mrs	54,89,93
Bannister & Co.	87
Bates W	24,47,49,68,71
Beaumont Admiral Sir Lewis	70
Beeching A	24,49,71
Belgium	9,10
Bennett Mrs L	47
Best T W	34
Bevan B Y	25,62,70,81
Bevan Mrs B Y	62,103
Bevan R A	34
Bevan Miss E	65,89,92
Black Sea	12
Blunt's Wood	24,
Bone Pte J	57,68
Borde Hill Estate	61,85,
Botting L/Cpl G	73,74,75,76,78,79,80
Botting Mrs D M	73,74,76,77,78,79
Bowell L/Cpl C	68,80
Bradley & Vaughan	69
Bristow Miss E	91,94
Britain, British Army, BEF etc.	9,10,11,12,13,14,16,17, 18,19,42,43,58,82,83,95,96,98,99
Broad Street	21,22,73
Brook Street	21,22
Brougham Mrs	92
Browne A	47
Burgess Hill Congr'tional Church	30
Burgess Hill	25,30,46,47,50,68,70,85
Burgess Hill Urban District Council	70
Burtenshaw B	24,47,49
Byng General	96
Caffyn S	24,49,93
Caffyn Miss K	71
Calais	11,
Cambrai	91,96,97,98,100
Campion Colonel W H	70
Canadian Forces	58,95
Caporetto	96
Card Pte T	53
Carling Dr Esther	66
Carter D	90
Carter J	90
Cartner H	31
Champagne	13,14,83
Chapman W P	89
Cheale Mrs	91
Chemin des Dames	11,58
Chichester	21,101
Children's Country Holiday's Fund	69
Chinnery A	48,68,80
Chute Ellis Mrs	91
Clarke Mrs S	92
Cleare Miss W	47,94
Cleare Mrs	30,31
Cleaver Mrs	66
Congregational Church	21,22,30,34,47,91,94,105
Constantine, King of Greece	59,82
Cook Pte C	52,53
Cooper Mrs R	90
Copyhold Cottage	89
Coronel, Battle of	11
Crawley	21
Creche, Richmond Villa	39,
Croucher A	24,46,47,49,52,89,
Cuckfield Church Bellringers	48
Cuckfield Food Control Committee	71,90
Cuckfield Gas Works	26,46
Cuckfield Infant Welfare Centre	65,66
Cuckfield Nursing Association	65
Cuckfield Park	22,25,39,53,55,61,65,103
Cuckfield Rural District Council	22,25,26,40
Cuckfield School	48,61,67,72
Cuckfield Urban District Council	22,25,26,27,30,35,37,46,49, 52,55,56,69,71,85,87,88,90,91,
Cuckfield War Saving Association	29,91
Cuckfield Women's Suffrage Society	50,91
Dancy E Mrs	52
Dancy E	80
Dardenelles	12
Dengate Miss D	63
Denman J	24,46,47,49
Denny Mrs	92
Denyer V	31
Ditty Box, The	79
Divall F	31
Donne F	27,41
Drill Hall	28,89
East Prussia	10
East Sussex Agricultural Committee	24,56
East Surrey Regiment	52
Eastern Front	12,82
Egypt	57,68,99
Ellis Robert	66

106   A SMALL TOWN AT WAR

Falkenhayn General	17
Falkland Islands	11
Flanders	58,59,72,83,95,99,105
Flesquieres	96
Flint Oliver	66
Fox W T	24
France, Army etc.	9,10,11,13,17,18,42,58,82,96,99,105
Fuller Mrs	91
Germany, Army etc	9,11,12,13,14,17,18,19,42,43,58, 83,95,96,97,98,105
German Navy	11,18,19
German Spring Offensive	105
Gibb Miss L M	28
Gibson R	48
Gibson A	71
Gill Miss	91
Gladmaan Pte H	86
Glanusk Lady	66
Gneisenau	11
Godman Mrs	50
Godsmark Alice	103
H M S Good Hope	11
Haig Field Marshall Douglas	17,29,58,82,96
Haywards Heath	21,22,24,28,30,67,69,86,89,
Haywards Heath Building Society	33
Haywards Heath Magistrates Court	33,72
Haywards Heath U D C	22,25,30
Henley E	31
Henley T	80
Herrington W	35,48,67,69,81
Hindenberg Line	43,58,96,105
Hobson C	48
Holden A	80
Hollweg Bethman	19,82
Holy Trinity (Parish Church)	21,30,31,47,48,80,92,94
Hounsell F Snr	48,56
Hounsell F Jnr	48
Huckett Mrs	47
Huckett Miss	92
Hulls Miss	33
Hurstpierpoint	69
Huth Mrs	92
International Stores	34,71,87
Italian Forces, Campaigns etc	18.96
Jerusalem Campaign	92,96,99
Joffre, General	13,19
Jubilee Cottages	73
Jutland, Battle of	18
Keep L/Cpl A	31,60
Keep Daisy (Rhodes)	60,62
Kenny-Herberbert Major A H	34,69,70
King's Head	24,49
Kitchener Field Marshall Earl	12,19
Kleinwort Lady	92
Knight S	24,47,49,52,88
Knight Fred	47,94
Knight Frank	67
Knight Gnr W	86
Knott Mrs E	34
Kressenstein General	43
Kut	39,43
Lampson Mrs	89
Langemark	83
Lawson Winifred (Woolven)	61
Lens	14
Leyton House	38,62
Lindfield	21
Line A	90
Lister Major	26
Lloyd George David	14,19
London Gazette	72
Loos	14
Lyon E	31
Machine Gun Corps	33,86
Maddock Reverend S	30,31,45,67,91
Maddock mrs	47,65
Malin Eva	61
Mansbridge Alice	66
Markwick Pte T	72
Marne, Battle of (River)	10,11,99
Martin Sapper H	46
Maude General	96
Mayfield House	63
Mays A	90
McClaren F	26
McConnell Dr	51
Menin Road Bridge	83,100
Mertens Reverend R H	81
Mesopotamia	12,18,19,38,39,84,96,98
Messines, Battle of	59,83,99
Mid Sussex	16,72,77,86,95
Mid Sussex Times	23,24,25,28,33,34,37,38,40, 45,46,48,49,52,54,61,64, 65,66,69,71,73,80,85,86,90,92
Middlesex Regiment	68
Miles G	47
Ministry of Food	40,51,92,93
Ministry of Munitions	14,39
Mitchell Alice M	103
Mitchell Cpl E	38,53,68
Mitchell Miss F	47
Mitchell F	48
Mitchell F E	48
Mitchell T	48
Mitchell William H	52,80
Mitchell W Holford	80
H M S Monmouth	11
Mons	10,99
Morfee P	31
Munro General	12
Murrell Mrs	24,67
Murrell G	80
Murrell L/Cpl H	93
Napper E	24,47,49
National Baby Week	54,55,65,67
National Patriotic Fund	69
National Service	34,44,52,103
Neuve Chappelle	13
Nicholas II Tsar of Russia	43
Nivelle General	42,58
Nivelle Offensive	42,58
Operation Alberich	43
Osbourne Pte G	53

Owen Wilfred	14,15,43,80,98,103
Palmer Sgt L	72
Paris	10,103,105
Parish Magazine	56,73,93
Parish Room	29,30,34,51
Passchendaele	14,59,83,95,100
Payne Miss E	24,34,47,49,65,91
Payne, Family	34,91
Pearse C	47
Pennefold A	67,80
Philpott Charles	81
Picture Theatre	28,29,54,89
Plan 17	13
Plumer General	59
Poelcappelle	84
Poland	12
Polygon Wood	83,100
Pozieres	72
Preston E M	25,30
Prestom Mrs	39,51,53,55,65,66,89
Punch Magazine	11,25,43,54,66
Queen's Hall	22,26,30,35,37,52,62,66,70
Quin Gladys	66
Quin Violet	66
RSPB	49
Randle Charles	11
Rapley A T	28,35
Rapley Reginald	66
Rate Mrs	92
Redwood May	66
Reeve Percy	72
Reeve Mrs N	72
Reeves W	90
Reichstag	19
Reid Capt S	57,72
Reid Mrs	62,65,93
Rhodes Sgt Major	72
Ridley James	66,80
Rist Mrs	66
Robinson W	47
Robins Mrs Elizabeth	51
Romania	18
Rowland F	31
Rowland James	48
Rowland Pte J	87
Royal Berkshire Regt	34,72
Royal Engineers	38,68,86,88
Royal Field Artillery	86
Royal Flying Corps	52
Royal Fusiliers	93
Royal Marines Light Infantry	73,77
Royal Navy	11,18,19,98
Royal Sussex Regiment	33,53,57,72,87,93,99,100
Royal Warwickshire Regiment	87
Royal West Kent Regiment	72
Rural Deanery of Cuckfield	21
Russia, Army etc.	7,9,14,82,96
S S Luisitania	14
Salonika	18,52,85,98
Salter Mrs C	103
Salvation Army	30
Sassoon Siegfried	18,20,41,57,59,84,88,94
Scharnhorst	11
Schlesinger Mrs	92
Schlieffen Plan	12
Selby Mrs	66
Selby Sgt A	72
Selby L/Cpl P	87
Serbia	9,10
Sergison Capt. C W	55,66
Ship Inn	24,53
Somme, Battle of	14,17,18,29,40,59,99,100
Southern Belle	24
Sparrow Club	49
Staplefield	22
Stevens W	30
Stevens 2nd Lt F.	52
Symons T I	24,47,49
Taylor A B	70
Tidey Norah	66
Tincler C	80
Tree Pte A	86
Tribunals	26,31,32,34,55,56,72
Trotter R	85
Turkey, Ottoman Empire, Army etc.	9,12,39,43,82,84,96
Turner Mrs	66
Turner Harcourt	80
Turner Miss	91
Turner Capt M	93
Upton L/Cpl L	86
VAD Hospital	22,28,37,38,54,61,67,70,89,103
Vaughn Mrs	47
Verdun	17,18,42
Vimy Ridge	14,58,96,100
Voller Mabe	66
Voluntary Work Organisation	47
War Hospital Supply Depot	22,39,47,103
Waugh C H	24,25,26,33,46,47,49
Webb J	90
Webber Charles	11
Wells Tom	73,89
Wells Mrs	92
Wesleyan Chapel	21,47
West Hylands (Board of Guardians etc.)	22,33,47,91,92
Western Front	11,43,95,96,105
Wheale A	45
Whiteman's Green	21,22,39,52,62
Whyte Gabrielle	82
Wilsman S	90
Wilson President Woodrow	19
Wilson Reverend C W G	26,31,32,34,48,80,104
Wilson Mrs	47,65
Witham Mrs E	57
Women's Institute	50,91,104
Women's Land Army	44,61
Wood 2nd Lt D	72
Wood Lt S	88
Woods G	48
Worsley R	28
Worsley Lt R S	52
YMCA	30,31,45
Young Pte J	72
Ypres	58,82,83
Ypres, First Battle of	11,13,99
Ypres, Third Battle of	59,72,83,95,100